Praise for *Your Spirit Will Soar*

"*Your Spirit Will Soar* is a wonderful companion for those moments that come to us when we feel stuck or uncertain on our creative journey. It gives us a selection of empowering exercises, both written and visual, in which we can gain clarity about who we are and where we most want to go. It can be a guide to creative freedom."

—Cat Bennett, artist and author

"*Your Spirit Will Soar* is a life guide for a deep inner exploration. Peyton invites you to birth your dreams through proven creative exercises to open your heart and mind and to say, "yes!" to the dreams that are uniquely yours."

—Susyn Reeve, author, mentor, and creative

"The workbook flows like a creative journal for the senses. We are guided to connect to parts of ourselves that are reminiscent of our inner child—full of creative power and possibility. As a trauma therapist trained in the expressive arts I would recommend this workbook to my clients. It provides a joyful, powerful canvas for play and discovery. If you are looking for a deep guided self exploration tool this workbook is it!"

—Gabriela Cristina Celeiro, MSW, LCSW

"Filled with divine intention and practical, loving exercises, this workbook helps its reader find their own inner wisdom. Peyton's own creativity and clarity infuse this workbook with gentle guidance for experienced practitioners as well as those looking to begin trusting their intuition. If you are looking for ways to tune in, refine your vision, and feel connected to Spirit (whatever that means for you), I can't recommend this book enough! I can see myself going back to it again and again over the years."

—Shari Caplan, poet

Your Spirit Will *Soar!*

A Creative Workbook to Awaken Your Wildest Dreams

Created by Peyton Pugmire
www.creativespiritma.com

Thank You

to the following creative spirits for their input, inspiration, and support:

Barbara Hoffmann, PhD (editor)
Gabriela Celeiro, LCSW
Susyn Reeve, author, mentor, and creative
Cat Bennett, artist and author
Michael Trotta, coach and storyteller
Saphira Linden, drama therapist and author
Shari Caplan, poet
Karina Klehm, healer
Stephanie DeFazio, spreader of joy
Jennifer Earls, dancer and coach
Melissa Stacey, queen of organizing
Andy Cahill, coach
and
James Ashton, sailor, minister, and my beloved husband

"Row, row, row your boat
gently down the stream.
Merrily, merrily, merrily, merrily,
life is but a dream."

-children's song by Eliphalet Oram Lyte

Table of *Contents*

Dear Creative Spirits ix

The Sky's the Limit! x

Warm-Ups 1

    Mesmerizing Mandalas 2

    Hatching from Within 6

    Your Soul Powers! 8

    Life Review 16

    Acrostic Poems 29

Self-Care and Acceptance...35

    Inner Sanctuary Haiga 36

    Your Personal Season 40

    Inner Child Pen Pals 45

    Keys to the Kingdom 48

Positive Mindset 51

    Become a Joy Magnet! 52

    Yin and Yang: Your Shadow and Light 53

    Thirty Quotes for Inspiration! 57

Intuitive Guidance 59

    Design Your Own Oracle Cards! 60

    Intuitive Chakra Coloring 66

Dreams, Passions,and Goals 77

    Draw Your 'Soul-ogo' 78

    Write Your 'Soul-ogan' 79

    Personal Myth 80

    Come Out Everyday 91

Table of *Contents*

Your Higher Self 97

    Out of the Rainbow 98

    Your Sacred Duality 104

Final Activities (for now) 117

    A Month of Affirmations! 118

    Write Your Eulogy 121

    Create Your Own Ceremony! 126

    Start a Soaring Spirits Circle! 129

Dear creative spirit,

This workbook is designed to help stir your imagination and awaken your truth, dreams, and passions! It is my hope that these activities inspire you and help you connect with peace, love, and joy for all that you are. Perhaps you are seeking clarity around your sense of purpose or maybe you're in need of a deeper connection with your heart and soul. This book can help!

You will become a channel for your inner wisdom and sacred authenticity when you engage in these exercises. As you create, be open to the voice of your heart and the clarity that emerges from within yourself. Trust your intuition and allow your critical brain to chill out for a while (it'll be just fine!). What you do in this book can open doorways to exciting and creative adventures. So, have fun and enjoy the journey!

A message for those using this book to explore their passions and sense of purpose: Our greatest passions and wildest dreams do not have to be our day job for which we receive a paycheck. They certainly can, but if one never receives a penny for them, this does NOT devalue your dreams. Following our bliss is soul medicine that requires no remuneration, for it is through these divine efforts that we ultimately nourish ourselves and the entire world.

With love and admiration for all that you are,
Peyton Pugmire, artist, teacher, guide

The *Sky's* the Limit!

Here are some suggestions on how to make the most of these exercises.

Take Your time: These exercises can take you deep within yourself, so move at your own pace. It is ok if you do not complete an exercise in one sitting.

Choose Your Own Adventure: I recommend doing the final chapter's exercises after you have done all or most of the others. Besides that, there is no prescribed sequence, so work through the exercises in order or skip around.

Supplies: Gather pens, pencils, crayons, markers, and more! Use separate paper if you wish to write and draw outside of the actual workbook.

Make it Sacred: Light a candle. Brew a cup of tea. Play soft music. Prepare your space and approach this work in ways that feel reverent to your heart and soul.

Creative Possibilities: These exercises can be expanded upon in many ways. An exercise might inspire a step that I have not offered, so keep going! Be a creative rebel: draw when I say write, and vice versa. Or collage or paint! Put on music and move your body. It's up to you! And that's the point.

Processing: Take time after each exercise to consider what has emerged from within yourself and on the page. I've provided journal pages for most of the exercises to help you process. You can respond to these in the workbook or in a separate journal.

Process Not Perfection: This is NOT about creating artistic masterpieces, and no one needs to see the contents of your workbook. This is a safe space. No judgement!

Re-Dos: You can re-do the exercises again and again since they are designed to reflect your present state. We are ever-changing, like the seasons, and so your responses will change each time you engage with the work. Feel free to make copies of pages for your future use.

Visualizations: Some exercises require you to close your eyes and imagine something special before you create. I have provided scripts for these guided meditations. Record the scripts electronically or have a friend read them aloud to you so that you may fully immerse yourself in the visualization.

Power in Numbers: Consider doing the exercises with a friend or in a small group. This can provide accountability and support as you journey inward. See my suggestions in the back of the book on how to start a Soaring Spirits Circle!

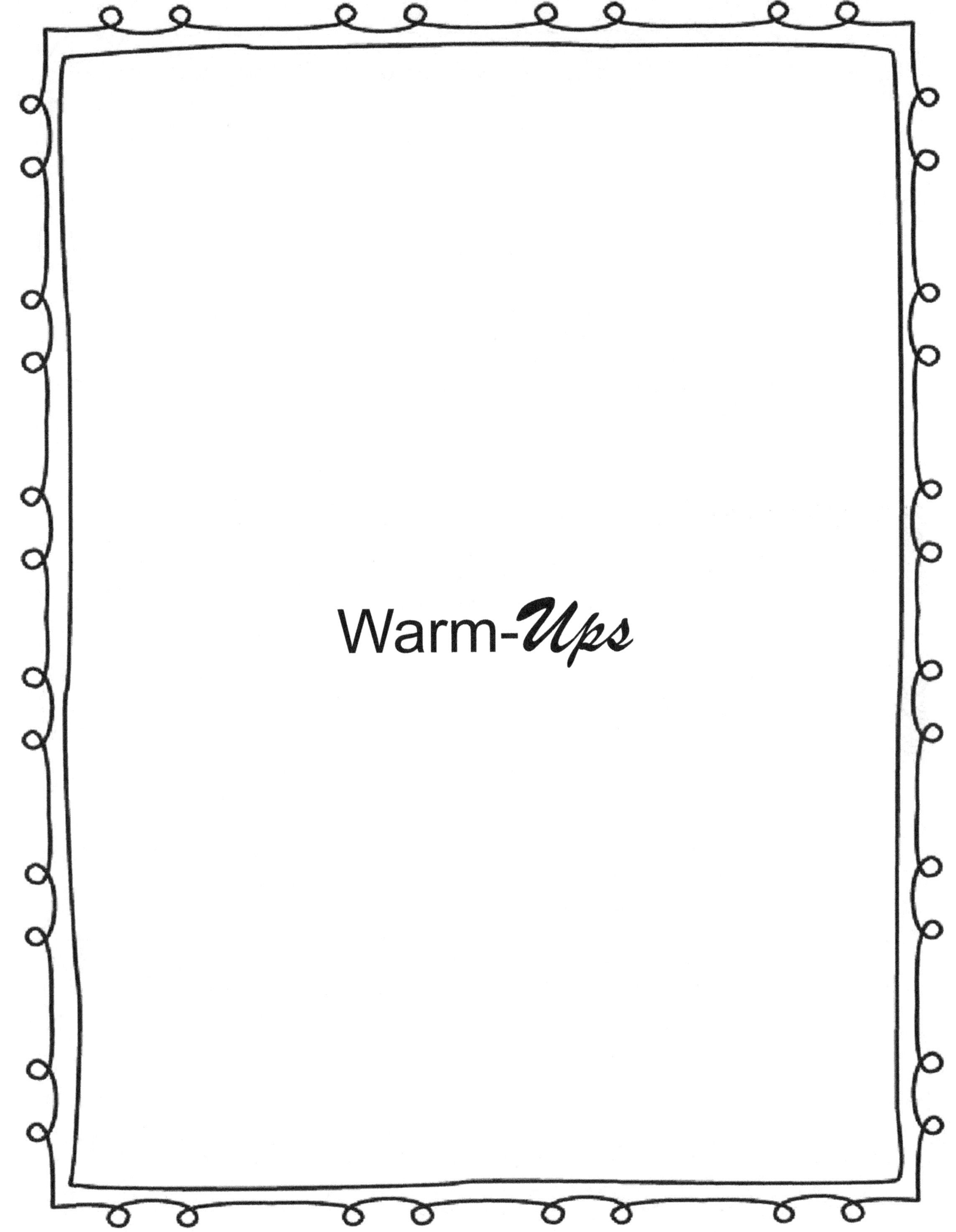

Warm-Ups

Mesmerizing *Mandalas*

'Mandala' is the Sanskrit word for circle. These circular works of art represent one's spiritual journey starting from the outside and moving towards the center through many layers. A mandala is also a tool for meditation, and it can help create within us feelings of peace and calm. Their visual beauty, too, is a source of creative inspiration. .

For this first warm-up exercise, you are invited to immerse yourself in the beauty and power of mandalas. The first two mandalas require your artistic touch, so grab your colored pencils and color away! The third mandala—a blank one—is yours to create from scratch. Use the first two as inspiration or pull ideas from your own imagination. I like to work from the center and work my way out towards the outer edge. Your design can include whatever kinds of images, symbols, and marks that you'd like. You can even incorporate words.

Here are some suggestions:

- Light a candle and create a sacred space in which to work. Be sure to turn off your phone, too.

- Treat this process like a meditation, and use your completed mandalas as visual meditation tools. Allow calm and peace to enter your heart and mind as you color and create.

- Create an ephemeral (temporary) nature mandala. Go outside and collect leaves, sticks, flowers, bark, stones, and more to create a mandala on the ground. Do this with a friend (try doing it in silence), and then allow the finished mandala to erode naturally.

Color the *Mandala*

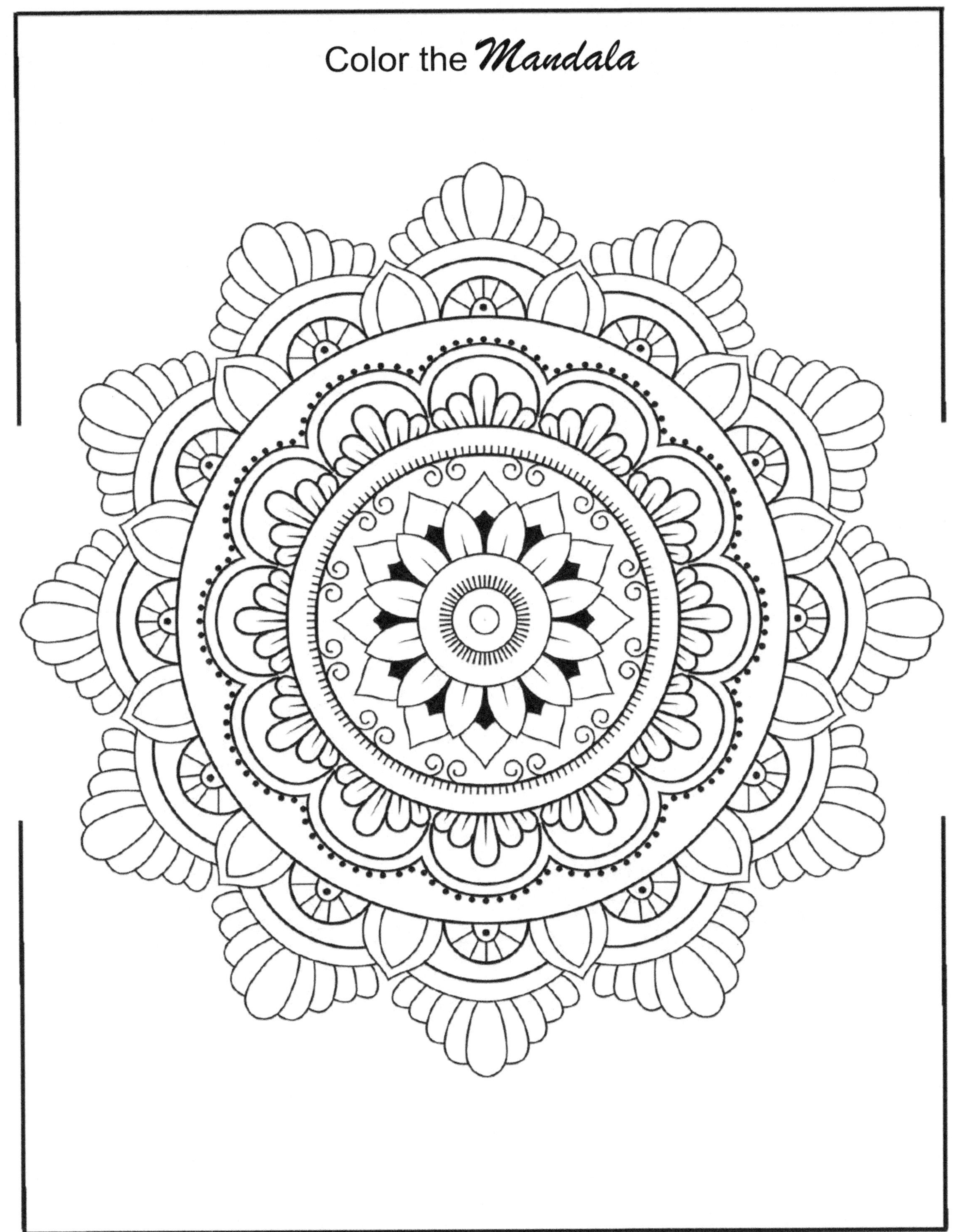

Color the *Mandala*

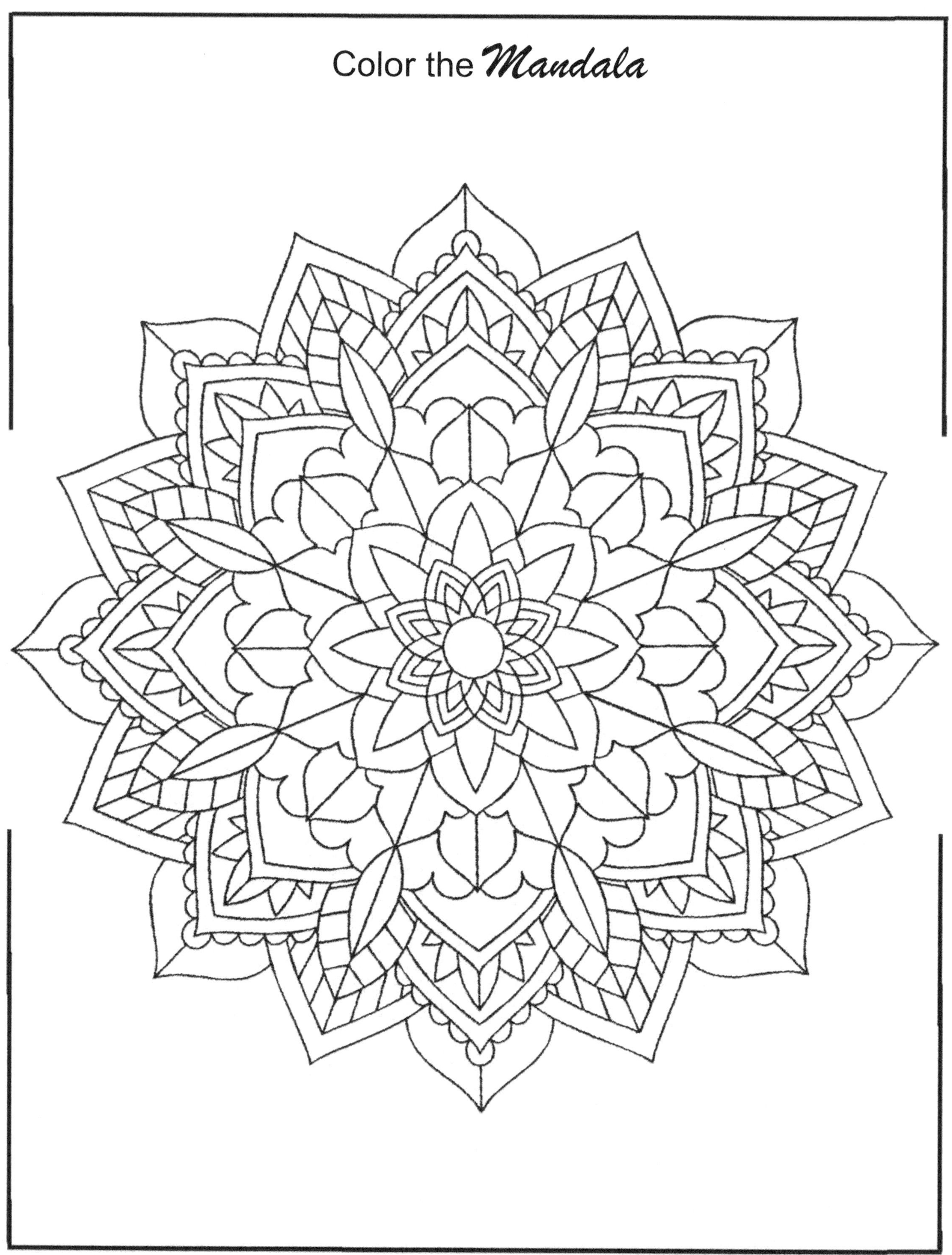

Create Your Own *Mandala*

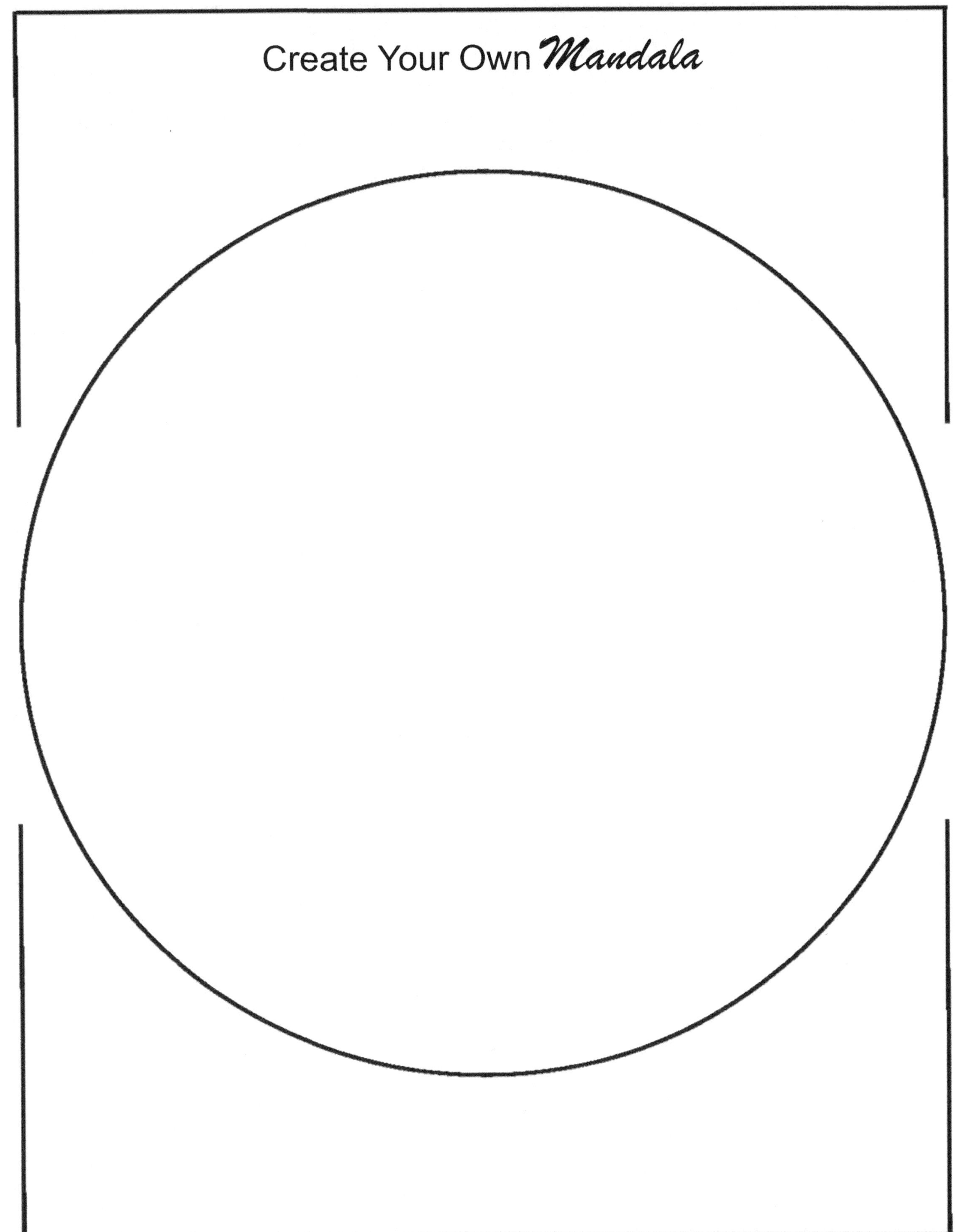

Hatching from Within

Draw and color a cracked egg and what is coming out of it. It can be whatever you like including anything that realistically does not come from an egg (example: a car).
The only rule is that you CANNOT draw a baby chick.

Hatching from Within Journal

1. How is your drawing a reflection of you? What is 'hatching' or wanting to emerge in your life these days?

2. How do you feel about this?

3. Is there a call to action from your drawing?

4. What does the hatched item need to be nurtured?

Your *Soul* Powers!

Your Soul Powers are your most pleasurable passions, qualities, and actions. They create instant feelings of joy and peace within you and inspire you to engage fully in your life and the world around you.

When we honor our Soul Powers and incorporate them into our daily lives, we feel a sustained sense of purpose and aliveness.

This warm-up exercise is focused on helping you identify your own Soul Powers. You also will be guided to return to your list of Soul Powers for other exercises in the book.

Here's a suggestion: If you find it difficult to come up with your own responses to the Soul Power questions, ask your loved ones, close friends, and mentors for their ideas about you. Those who love us and truly know us can sometimes be the best mirrors to reflect who we are.

Listing Your *Soul* Powers

Start with the left column and then do the right one. For the essence, tune in to what the absolute quality is of your response in the left column. Don't overthink the essence. It can be the same as your response in the left column. There are no wrong answers!

In this column list your responses to the question.	In this column write the essence of each response.
What do you love about yourself? *(personality traits, talents, skills, beliefs, etc.)*	
EXAMPLE: my sense of humor ⟶	laughing and having a good time
EXAMPLE: my love for life ⟶	joyful living
Whom do you love to spend your time with the most?	

Listing Your *Soul* Powers

What do you admire about children?

What brings you feelings of peace and calm?

What compliments do you often receive from others?

Listing Your *Soul* Powers

Listing Your *Soul* Powers

What do you love most about nature?

What do you value in a relationship?

What dreams do you hold?

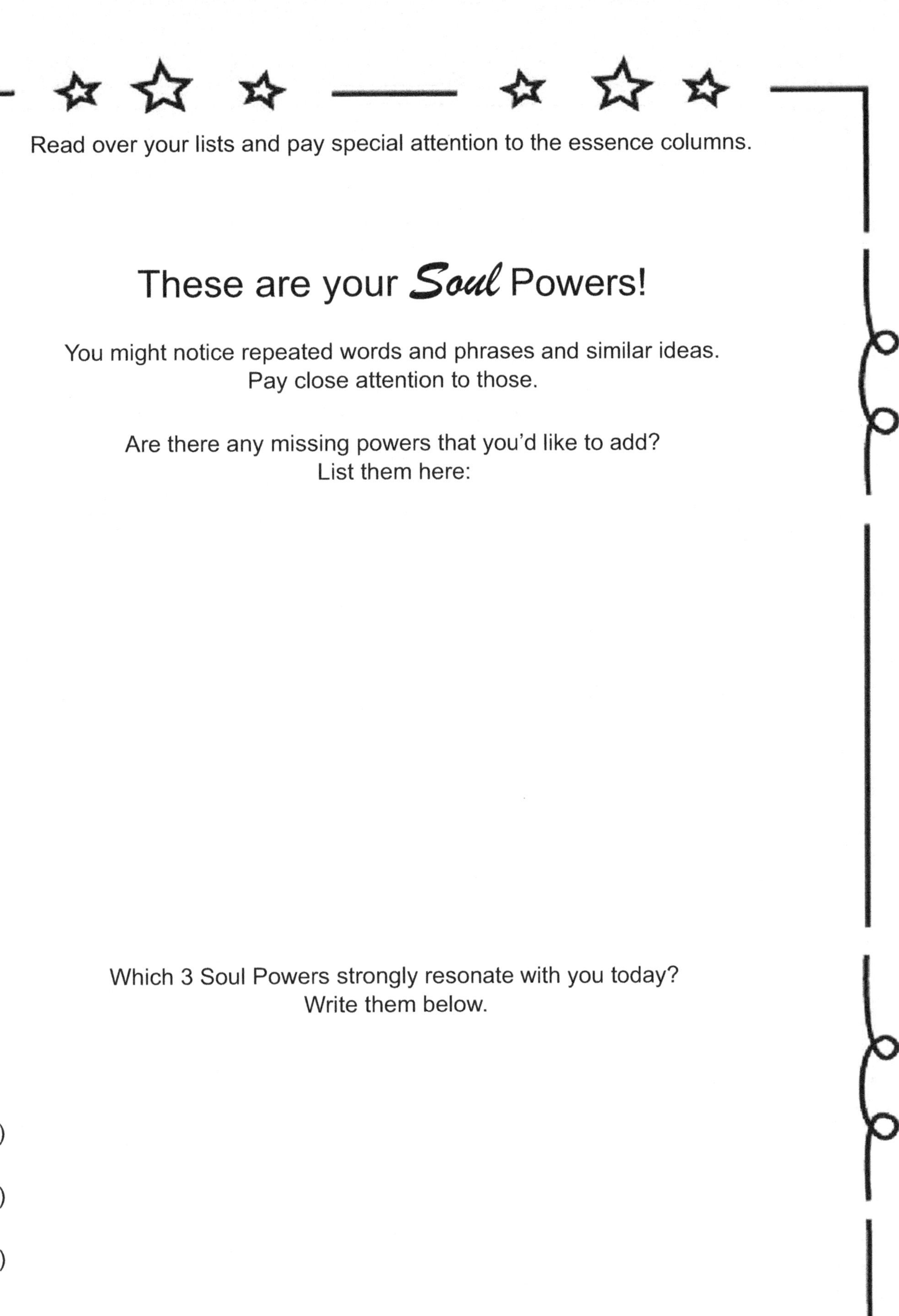

Read over your lists and pay special attention to the essence columns.

These are your *Soul* Powers!

You might notice repeated words and phrases and similar ideas.
Pay close attention to those.

Are there any missing powers that you'd like to add?
List them here:

Which 3 Soul Powers strongly resonate with you today?
Write them below.

1)

2)

3)

Soul Power Journal

1. How does it feel to have identified your Soul Powers? Any surprises?

2. How do your Soul Powers currently show up in your life?

3. How can they be a bigger part of your life? What support and resources do you need for this to happen?

4. Re-create your lists in 3 months. How have your Soul Powers changed? How can you honor your new Soul Powers?

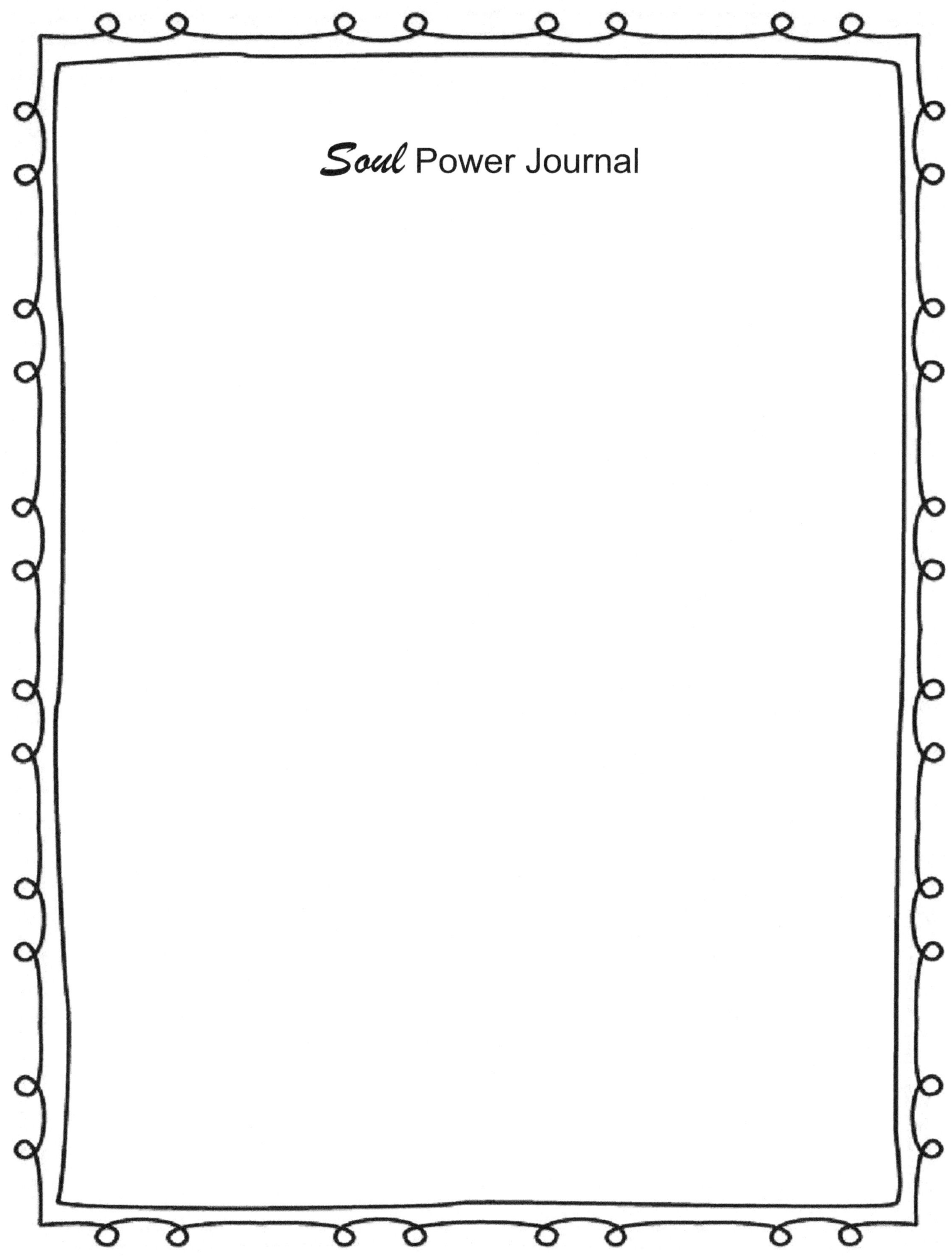

Soul Power Journal

Life Review

Reflecting on our life from birth, we can identify patterns and recall key moments in our personal history that changed us and made us into who we are today. Patterns can help remind us of our path and where we may desire further growth and learning.

Create your life review: On the following pages, list all significant experiences, happenings, occurrences, and incidents in your life history. Work decade by decade (up through your current age) so that you may more easily focus your memory recall. Consider ALL kinds of experiences that left some sort of imprint on your heart, mind, body, and soul.

Examples include schooling, social interactions, family events, hardships and losses, successes, hobbies, travels, jobs, rites of passage, and residential moves.

You may either make lists of each decade's events, or you can draw a horizontal timeline and fill in your memories along the graph. Your choice!

Its possible to feel many emotions in this process. This can be a meaningful result of this exercise. Move at your own pace, and take time to honor the feelings that emerge.

Before you begin, find a comfortable place to write, and then close your eyes. Take a few deep breaths. Set the intention to recall all that will be most helpful for you now. And then be open and go with the flow as you write. Work with what feels safe and helpful for you now.

Here's a suggestion: If listing memories by decade does not work for you, try organizing them in another way. For example, if you associate your early experiences with school levels, use those as your categories.

Life Review: Ages 1-10

Life Review: Ages 21-30

Life Review: Ages 41-50

Life Review: Ages 51-60

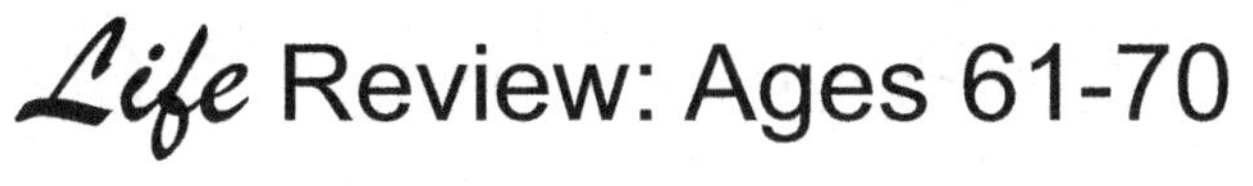

Life Review: Ages 61-70

Life Review: Ages 71-80

Life Review: Ages 91+

Life Review Journal

1. Read over your timelines and mark incidents that resonate with your current goals. For example, if you are desiring clarity around your life purpose, you might look for events that speak to that topic. Or, if you are doing emotional healing work, you might make note of the harder events in which you were hurt or hurtful to others. After you have done this, reflect upon patterns and meaning.

2. Honor a particular memory or decade. How do you feel about it now? How did you feel then? How did one incident shape your life back then, and how does it effect your current life? Journal about this or create inspired artwork.

3. Share your timeline or parts of it with a trusted love one. This, however, is not necessary. Only do so if it feels right for you.

4. Assign a movie-like title to each decade. Have fun and be creative! This might shed light on the overall meaning and lessons of that period in your life.

5. Celebrate yourself! How does it feel to look back over your many years of life experiences? Now, eat a yummy meal, put on some fabulous music, dance, or take a cozy bath. You deserve it!

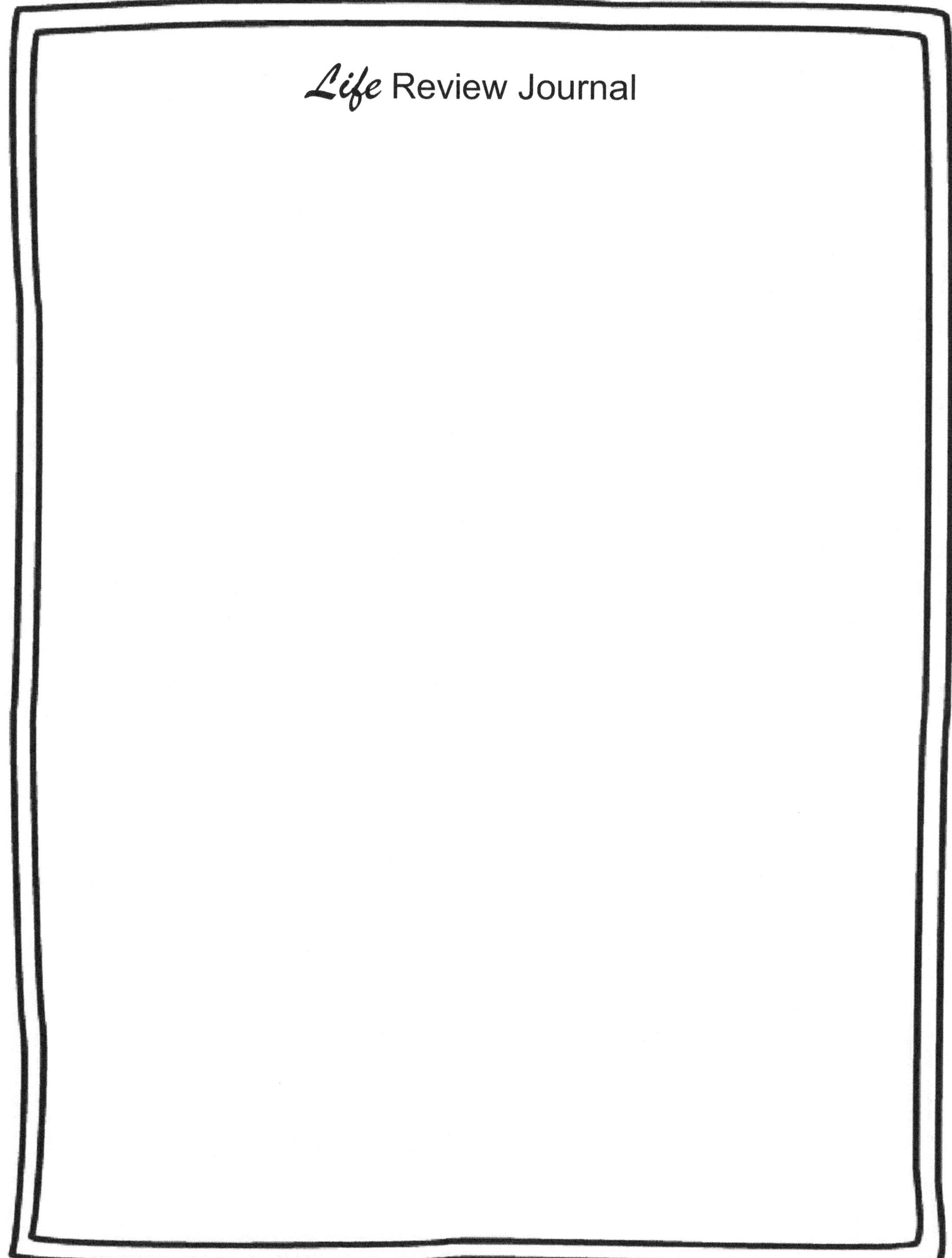

Life Review Journal

Acrostic *Poems*

Acros what…?! Acrostic poems are simple poems using a root word or phrase. The root word is written vertically. You then write one word or short phrase, horizontally, off of each root word letter. The root word's letters must start each horizontal word. These poems are simple AND meaningful! Here's an example using "hat" as the root word:

Happy heads
Adorned
Tastefully

Use the provided root words in this section to write some acrostic poems. Have fun and let your creative writing flow. If you'd like, choose your own root words, and go to town!

After you write each poem, draw and color a creative symbol or image that further expresses your poem's meaning.

Acrostic *Poem & Drawing*

Create your drawing in the extra space around the poem.

T
R
A
N
S
F
O
R
M
A
T
I
O
N

Acrostic *Poem & Drawing*

Create your drawing in the extra space around the poem.

I
M
A
G
I
N
A
T
I
O
N

Acrostic *Poem & Drawing*

Create your drawing in the extra space around the poem.

I
N
T
U
I
T
I
O
N

Acrostic *Poem & Drawing*

Create your drawing in the extra space around the poem.

H

E

A

R

T

A

N

D

S

O

U

L

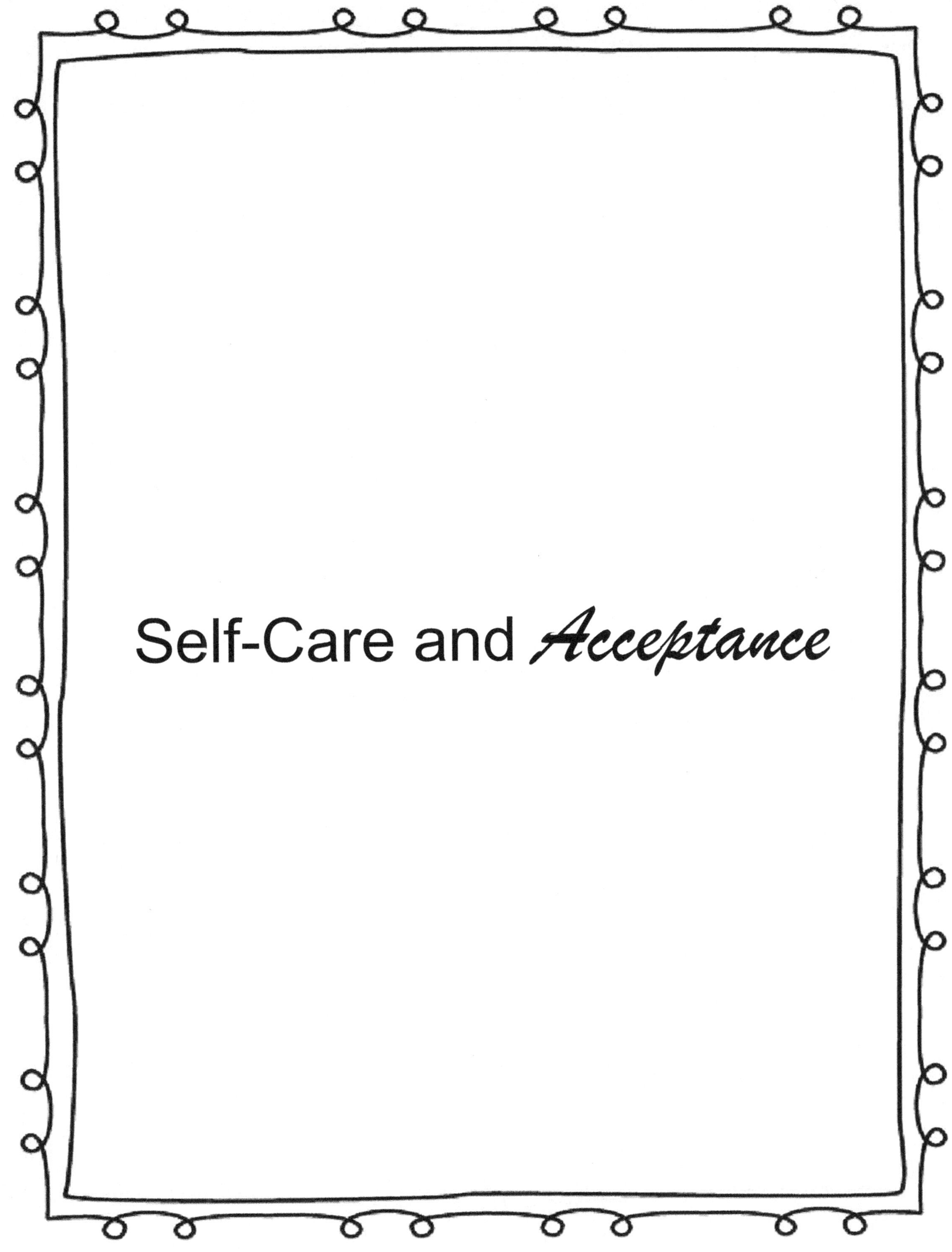

Self-Care and *Acceptance*

Inner *Sanctuary* Haiga

Like acrostics, haiku poems are also short and concise. When we pair haiku with illustration, it becomes a form of haiga, a Japanese art form that combines haiku with simple illustrative paintings. Haiku have a specific structure: They contain three lines. The first and third lines contain five syllables each, and the second line contains seven syllables.

For this exercise, you'll first visualize a special place (your inner sanctuary). Next, you'll write a haiku about your sanctuary and then create a drawing that further expresses your poem.

To start, get comfortable and take a deep breath. Next, imagine a beautiful, safe, and restorative place - any place that you wish: an enchanted forest, a chapel, a cabin beside a lake, a garden....anywhere, inside or outside, that feels good, safe, and nourishing for you now. This can be a place that really exists or one that you make up. Take a few moments in silence to connect with your sanctuary. Go there in your imagination. While visiting, use your inner senses to see, hear, smell, taste, and feel all that you can.

Next, write your haiku poem from <u>the point of view of your inner sanctuary</u>. What does it wish to express? Allow your imagination to lead the way and have fun! I've given you space to write two versions of your poem. Feel free to write more, if you'd like.

Finally, draw and color an image that illustrates and expresses the meaning of your haiku.

Inner *Sanctuary* Haiku (version 1):

Inner *Sanctuary* Haiku (version 2):

Inner *Sanctuary* Haiga Drawing

Incorporate your haiku text into the drawing.

Inner *Sanctuary* Haiga Journal

1.   How did it feel to journey to your inner sanctuary?

2.   How does your sanctuary exist in your life? Is it an imagined destination or an actual place?

3.   How do you benefit from visiting your sanctuary? How does it make you feel and what can you take with you when you leave?

4.   How can you incorporate your sanctuary's qualities into other facets of your life? How would you benefit from doing this?

Your Personal *Season*

Winter, spring, summer, and fall reflect our own natural cycles that we experience on emotional, physical, intellectual, and spiritual levels. Jobs can come and go, relationships can end, new inspiration arrives, joy pervades, and healing is ongoing. Like the seasons, we too are in a constant and dynamic state of flux. Nothing remains the same for too long. When we need it, change will come. Each season supports the next, and each quarter is necessary for the balanced whole. Consider the meaning of the seasons below:

Winter: A time for journeying within oneself for clarity and healing. A literal or symbolic death. A period of quiet rest. A restoration before the next rebirth. A hibernation and pause. The ground freezes and the white snow purifies the earth. The trees appear to die, and darkness sets in.

Spring: A time for rebirth and renewal. Feeling a sense of renewed energy, inspiration, and excitement for what lies ahead. A creative time to start something new with child-like energy. The trees blossom, and sunlight increases.

Summer: A time for complete embodiment of one's reality. Living full out. A maturation of what began in the spring. Outward interaction and lively engagement with others and the world around you. The trees' leaves are vibrant green, and the sunlight lasts long into evening.

Fall: A time for harvesting, completing the work, and celebrating your efforts. Preparing for a restful winter. The trees change color and shed all that which no longer serves them, and sunlight begins to wane.

Our personal season does not necessarily align with the actual calendar season. For example, our new job may have us feeling spring-like (when its actually winter), or the loss of a loved one might feel like you're headed into a personal winter of grief (when its actually July 12th).

For this exercise, tune into your current personal season. Next, write about it and then draw it. Complete the process by responding to the journal prompts.

Personal *Season* Free Write

Tune into one facet of your present life such as career, relationships, health, etc. Next, consider the four seasons. Which season resonates the most with your situation?

Set a timer for five minutes. After you hit start, write, write, write in response to the above question. Stop when five minutes has ended.

My life today is like the season ⎯⎯⎯⎯⎯⎯⎯⎯⎯⎯⎯⎯.

Personal *Season* Drawing

Inspired by your writing, draw your personal season. It can be as literal or as abstract as you'd like.

Personal *Season* Journal

1. How do you feel about your personal season? How do you wish to exist within it?

2. What guidance does the season provide in relation to your situation?

3. Consider the idea of cycles: Where have you come from, and which season is next? How do you imagine your situation in that next season?

4. What support do you need to exist peacefully in this current cycle?

5. How can you celebrate and honor your current season?

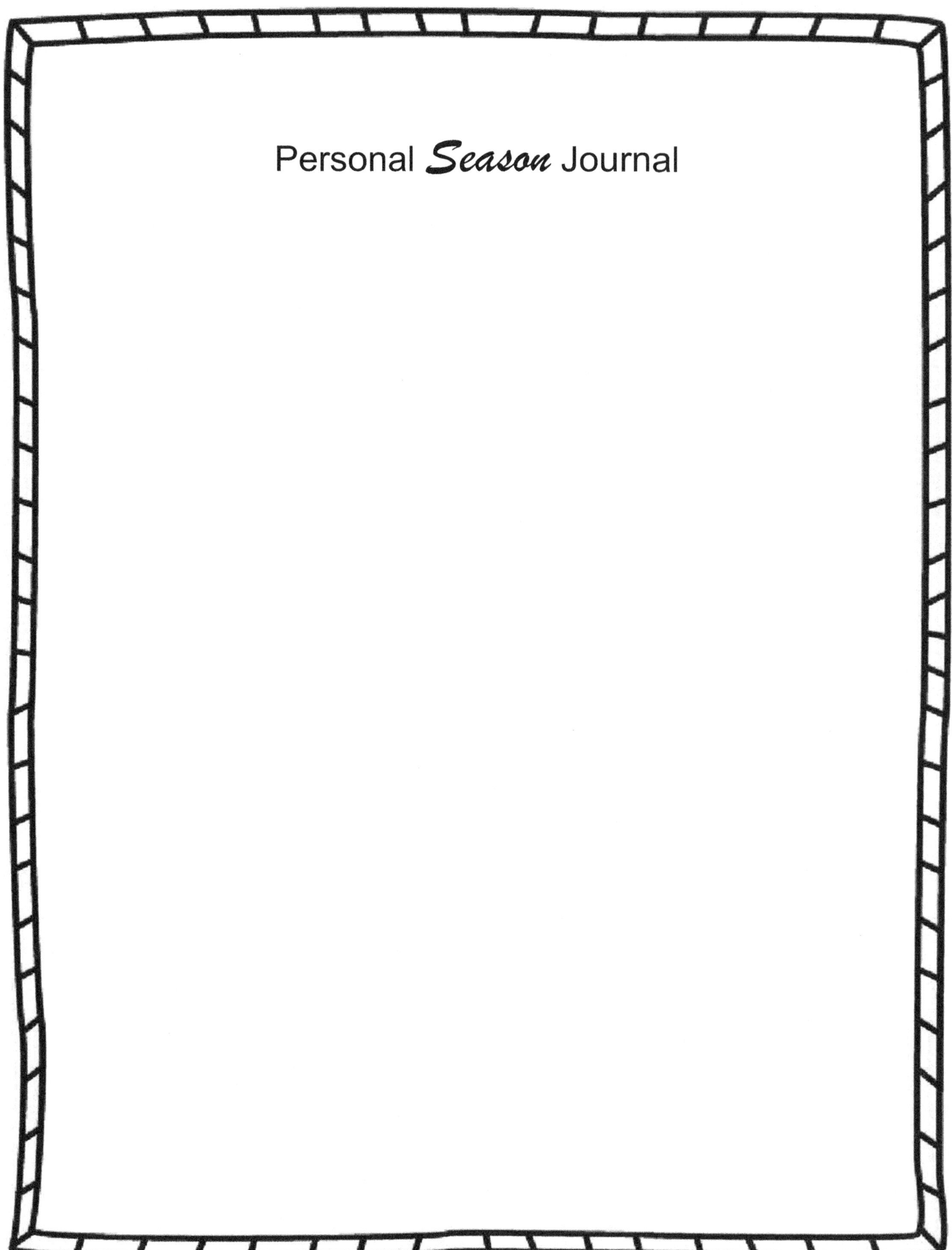

Personal *Season* Journal

Inner Child Pen Pals

Look back at your Life Review timeline, ages 1-10. Reread what you wrote and imagine your younger self. What about yourself then appeals to you now? What makes you curious? What can your younger self offer to you now?

First, find a comfy place to sit. Take a few deep breaths and imagine dropping down into your heart space. Invite your younger self to join you from within. When you're ready, write a letter from yourself to your child self. What do you wish to express, ask, request, and share?

After you have completed your first letter, write a second letter from your younger self to your current, older self. How would your younger self like to respond?

Here are some suggestions:

*   Write the letter from your younger self using your non-dominant hand. This is a powerful way of tapping your intuition, subconscious, and the right side of your brain (the creative side).

*   Find a photo of yourself from that age and take some time to examine it while you write your letters. Place the photo in a special spot as you write.

*   Seal the second letter in an envelope, stamp it, and address it to yourself. Give it to a trustworthy friend, and ask them to drop it in the mail at some unannounced time in the future—at least a month. Then await your dear pen pal's sweet letter!

Inner Child Pen Pals:

Letter to Younger Self

Date:

Dear ______________________,

Inner Child Pen Pals:

Letter to Older Self

Date:

Dear ___________________________,

Keys to the *Kingdom*

Imagine that you are the leader of a large kingdom like one in a fairy tale. You rule with kindness, wisdom, and creativity. Make a list of thirty things (practices, resources, objects, etc.) that you need on a regular basis in order to do the job in a healthy, joyful, and successful way. Imagine that everything and anything you need is at your disposal. Think holistically: What do you require emotionally, physically, intellectually, and spiritually?

1.	16.
2.	17.
3.	18.
4.	19.
5.	20.
6.	21.
7.	22.
8.	23.
9.	24.
10.	25.
11.	26.
12.	27.
13.	28.
14.	29.
15	30.

Keys to the *Kingdom* Journal

1. How did it feel creating this list (I hope you pushed yourself to think of all 30!)? Were there any surprises?

2. How are these needs a part of your life now? Which ones would you like to incorporate into your current routine?

3. What current habits would be replaced? Are you willing to make the shift?

4. What radical changes might occur if you were to make the shift?

5. As the leader of the kingdom with all of your needs fulfilled, how does your kingdom function? Are there specific occurrences that take place as a result of your fulfilled needs?

6. What is the name of your kingdom?

7. Draw, paint, or collage your thriving kingdom or draw yourself as its healthy, joyful, and successful leader.

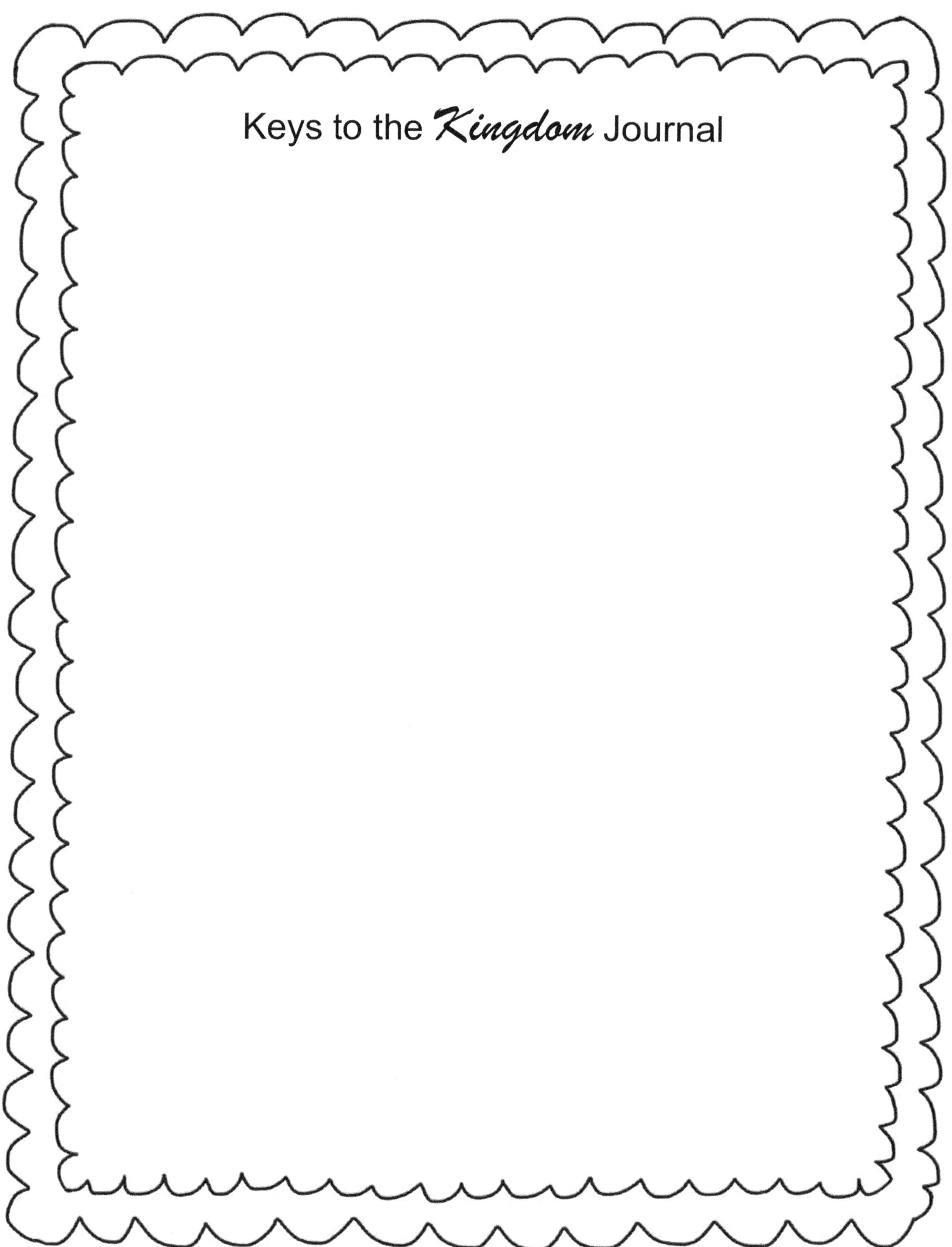
Keys to the *Kingdom* Journal

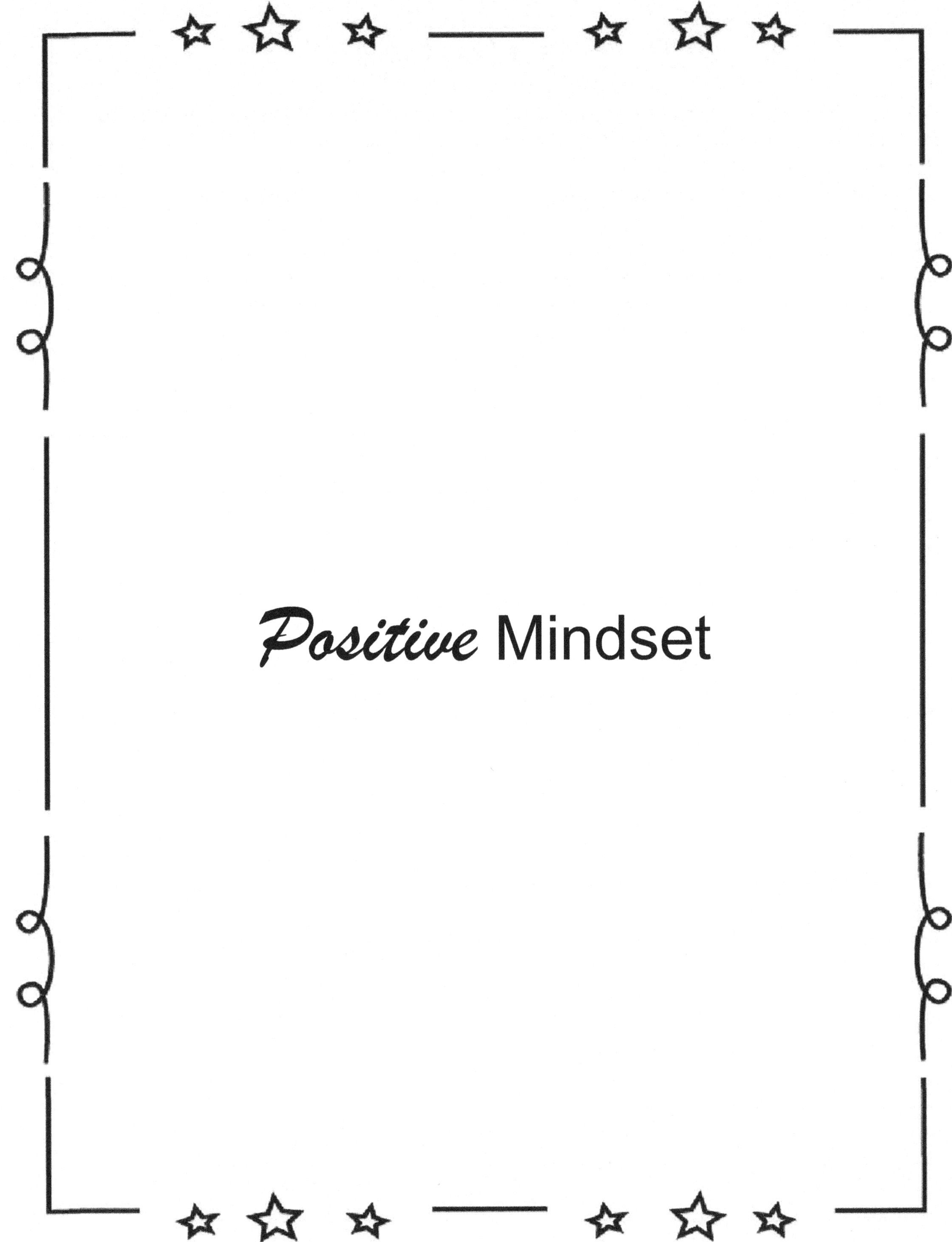

Positive Mindset

Become a *Joy* Magnet!

We become magnets for more goodness and joy when we acknowledge our gratitude for what we already have. This is due to the Laws of Attraction; like attracts like. On the flip side, when we focus on lack (fear), we're bound to attract more of that, too. So, be mindful! Our thoughts create our reality, and every external thing in our lives is a mirror reflecting back our inner reality.

So, let's become joy magnets! Make a gratitude list—all the things that you are grateful for in your life. Make your list below, and be sure to think of all thirty! This can also be a nice exercise to do with a loved one. You can do this in the morning or at night before falling asleep.
As the song goes, "count your blessings instead of sheep!"

1.	16.
2.	17.
3.	18.
4.	19.
5.	20.
6.	21.
7.	22.
8.	23.
9.	24.
10.	25.
11.	26.
12.	27.
13.	28.
14.	29.
15	30.

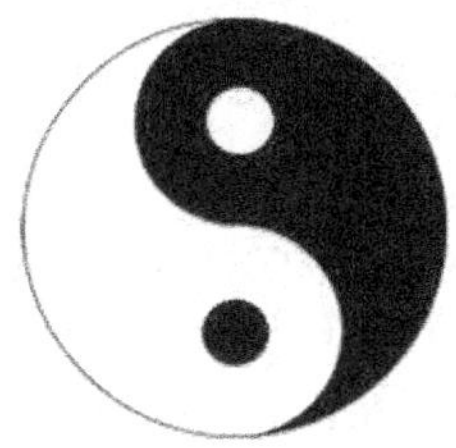

Yin and Yang:
Your Shadow and Light

Yin and yang, an ancient Chinese philosophical idea, states that shadow and light exist simultaneously in all living things. One does not exist without the other.

The yin and yang symbol (above) includes a black half (yin) representing the shadow, and the white half (yang) represents the light. Within each half are smaller circles of the opposite color, reminding us of the balanced and co-existing energies.

Our yin parts (shadow) are personal things that we find difficult about ourselves and others. We often ignore or criticize them and wrestle with them. Our yang parts are the things that we enjoy, love, and accept about ourselves and others.

More importantly, yin and yang are direct opposites of one another. Every shadow element has an opposite light element, and vice versa. This idea is embodied in the expression, "look on the bright side!" This suggestion invites us to look at the yang side of the yin. There is always a positive and love-filled opportunity in every difficult situation whether we choose to see it or not. When we do, we can transmute pain and mental anguish into peace, love, and even joy. Acknowledging both the yin and yang of our situations helps us to honor our wholeness.

In this exercise, you'll have the opportunity to consider the yin and yang of a current personal challenge.

Yin and Yang Drawing

Using the yin and yang symbol below, explore the shadow and light of a current challenge. For the sake of your drawing, the yin side (shadow) is not filled in with black. It contains the smaller circle labeled "yin."

In the yin side draw/color/write about your current challenge. Next, in the yang side, draw/color/write the positive opposites and invitations that your challenge presents. Fill it up and let it out! Re-create the symbol on larger paper if more space is desired.

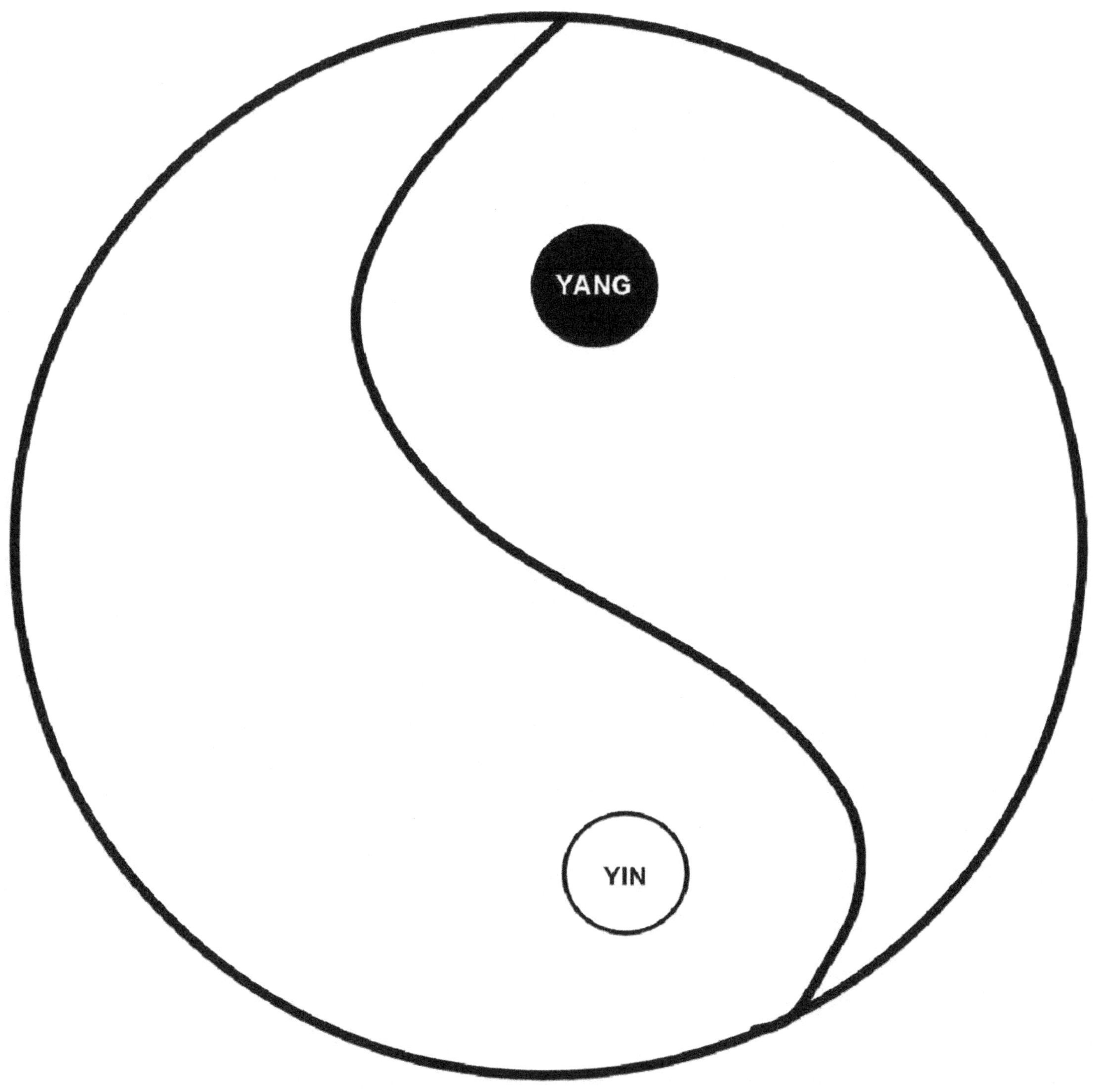

Yin and Yang Journal

1. How did it feel to express your yin?

2. How did it feel to express your yang?

3. From the yang side, what stands out? What appeals to you?

4. What radical positive shifts might occur if you were to act on them?

5. If forgiveness did not appear in your yang half, would you like to add it? If so, who or what needs forgiving? Does this include yourself?

6. Look back at your list of needs as the leader of your kingdom. In order to honor your yang, which needs will support your ability to do so? What else do you need for support?

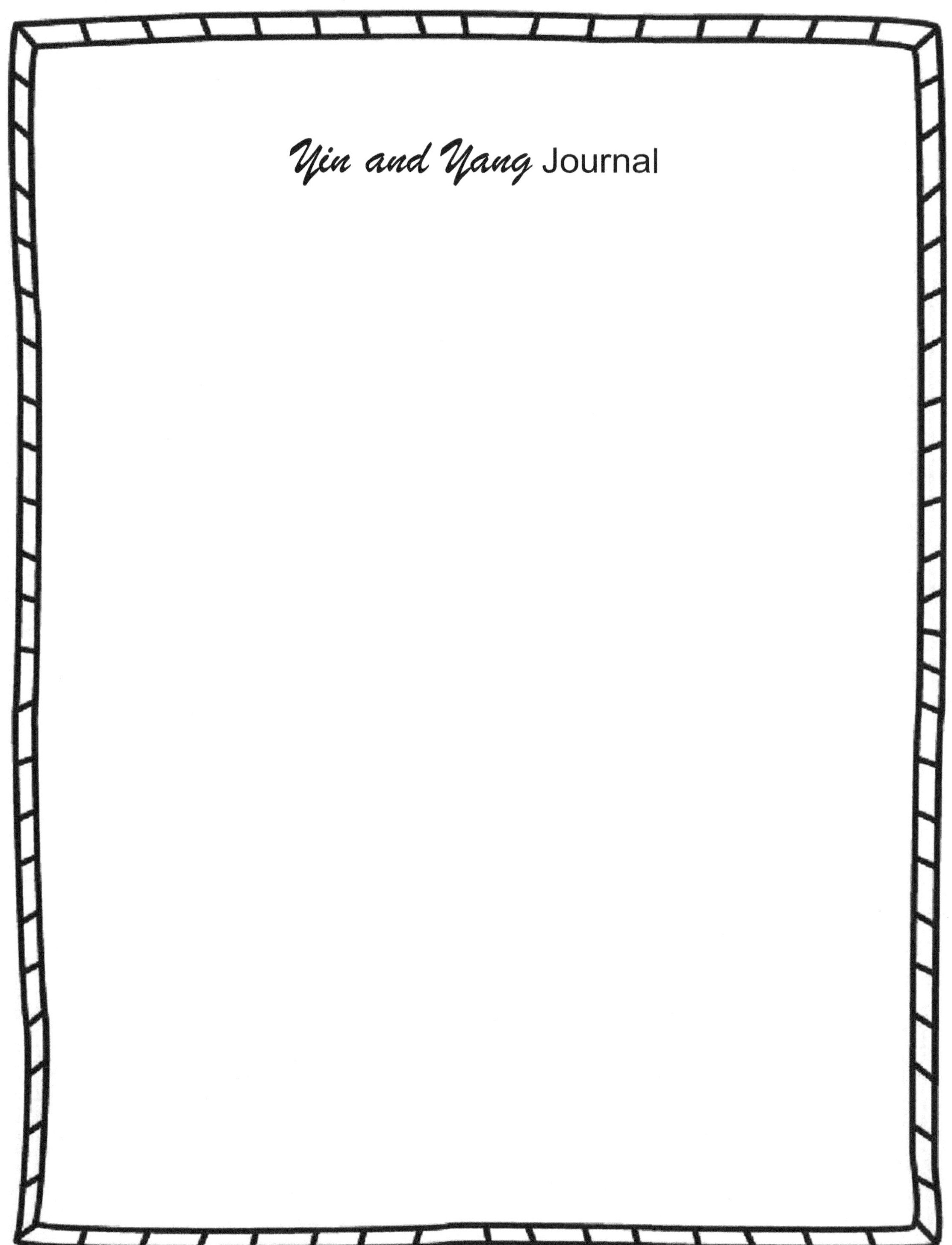

Yin and Yang Journal

Thirty Quotes for *Inspiration!*

Here are twenty-five quotes from great authors, poets, spiritual leaders, and artists. I have also left five spaces empty for you to add your own favorite quotes.

Make copies of the two pages of quotes, including the five you add. Next, cut the quotes into individual strips and fold them. Place them in a bowl, and place it in a special spot where you'll see it every morning. Intuitively select one quote each day for one month. Consider its meaning throughout your day. How does it apply to your goals, dreams, and present circumstances? Journal about its meaning — create a piece of inspired artwork — or discuss the quote with a friend over dinner. Enjoy the abundant wisdom!

"The universe buries strange jewels deep within us all, and then stands back to see if we can find them." —Elizabeth Gilbert, author

"When you do things from your soul, you feel a river of joy within you." —Rumi, poet

"I am a soul of love. A heart of peace. A mind of stillness. A being of light." —Anonymous

"You use a glass mirror to see your face; you use works of art to see your soul."
—George Bernard Shaw, playwright

"When you feel a peaceful joy, that's when you are near truth ." —Rumi, poet

"Listen to your intuitive voice and find what passion stirs your soul." —Wayne Dyer, author

"Respond to every call that excites your spirit." —Rumi, poet

"We all have the capacity to allow the universal energy of love to use us for the highest good. That is why we are here: to remember love and allow it to move through us, heal us, and inspire us to serve." —Gabrielle Bernstein, author

"The only unique contribution that we will ever make in this world will be born of our creativity."
—Brene Brown, author

"Search for the answers in your own soul, in your own intuition, from your own guides."
—Terry Lynn Taylor, author

"Look inside yourself; everything that you want, you already are." —Rumi, poet

"Work in the invisible world at least as hard as you do in the visible." —Rumi, poet

More Quotes!

"The desire to know your own soul will end all other desires." —Rumi, poet

"As I unclutter my life, I free myself to answer the callings of my soul." —Wayne Dyer, author

"For all the qualities which we admire or loathe in the world around us are reflections from within."
—Alan Watts, philosopher

"For us to be fully human, the Child Within must be embraced and expressed."
—Lucia Capacchione, Ph.D., author

"Peace comes from within. Do not seek it without." —Buddha, spiritual leader and teacher

"Music in the soul can be heard by the universe." —Lao Tzu, spiritual leader and teacher

"Happiness is the absence of striving for happiness." —Lao Tzu, spiritual leader and teacher

"Re-examine all that you have been told…dismiss that which insults your soul." —Walt Whitman, poet

"You will see in the world what you carry in your heart." —Anonymous

"Think of yourself as a human magnet, constantly attracting what you speak, think and feel."
—Anonymous

"Less force, more allowing." —Cat Bennett, artist and author

"The key to solving problems or issues you don't want in your life is to increase self-love."
—Terry Lynn Taylor, author

"Go in the direction of our heart's desire, and begin. There's no journey if we don't hop onto the train." —Cat Bennett, artist and author

#26: ____

#27: ____

#28: ____

#29: ____

#30: ____

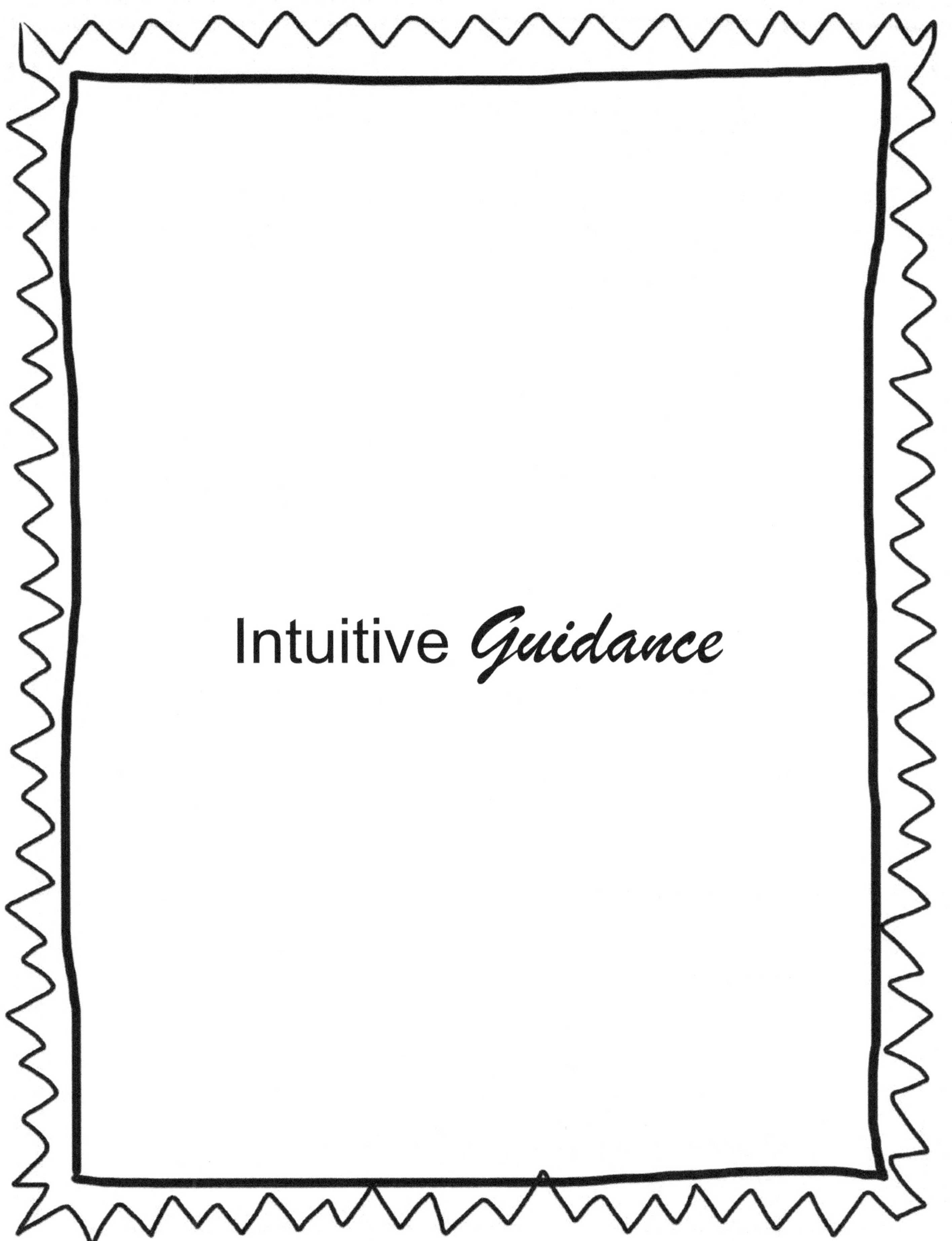

Intuitive *Guidance*

Design Your Own *Oracle Cards!*

My favorite divination tool are oracle cards. They coax my intuitive knowing, and so I use them regularly for guidance. I love the cards so much that I've even designed my own deck, the Oz Oracle Cards, inspired by the book <u>The Wonderful Wizard of Oz</u> by L. Frank Baum. Oracle cards come in a deck, and each card provides an inspirational message for the user. The cards' images and words stir our intuition, from which further guidance emerges.

Each deck has its own artistic style, and each card is designed around one positive message, which is expressed through the card's artwork. For example, a card with a message about love might include images of Cupid, hearts, or a blossoming rose. The word 'love' might also be included in the design. Each card is a beautiful work of art, and its symbolic images are intended to inspire new thoughts, feelings, and ideas within the reader.

Decks also come with a guide book containing the designer's own interpretation of each card. I believe, however, that the book is not necessary to benefit from the cards. All you need to do is tune into your own intuition and inner senses (everything you see, think, feel, and hear) as you examine each card, and THIS will result in not only a perfect reading but also one grounded in your own personal circumstances.

For this exercise, you will design three of your very own oracle cards inspired by your Soul Powers. The journal pages will then help you understand each of your card's powerful guidance.

Here are some suggestions:

- If you'd like examples of oracle cards before you begin, do some online research. There are tons of decks out there in the market.

- Do this work outside of the workbook, and collage your designs using glue and cut-outs from magazines.

- Photograph or scan your completed designs, re-size them, and turn them into actual cards! Keep creating, and make a full deck!

"

Oracle Card #1

Refer back to your list of Soul Powers. Choose one to inspire the design of your card. Draw and color the card's design inside the outline below. **Suggestions:** Fill the space entirely (no white space), and use primarily images. Keep words and text to a minimum.

Oracle Card #2

Refer back to your list of Soul Powers. Choose one to inspire the design of your card. Draw and color the card's design inside the outline below. Suggestions: Fill the space entirely (no white space), and use primarily images. Keep words and text to a minimum.

Oracle Card #3

Refer back to your list of Soul Powers. Choose one to inspire the design of your card. Draw and color the card's design inside the outline below. Suggestions: Fill the space entirely (no white space), and use primarily images. Keep words and text to a minimum.

Oracle Card Journal

(use for each card)

1. What is the symbolic or literal meaning of each image in the card?

2. What images stand out the most to you? What is the guidance behind this attraction?

3. What feelings does the card evoke within you?

4. What do you 'hear' within yourself when you examine the card?

5. What other thoughts come to mind as you examine the card?

6. What is the card's call to action?

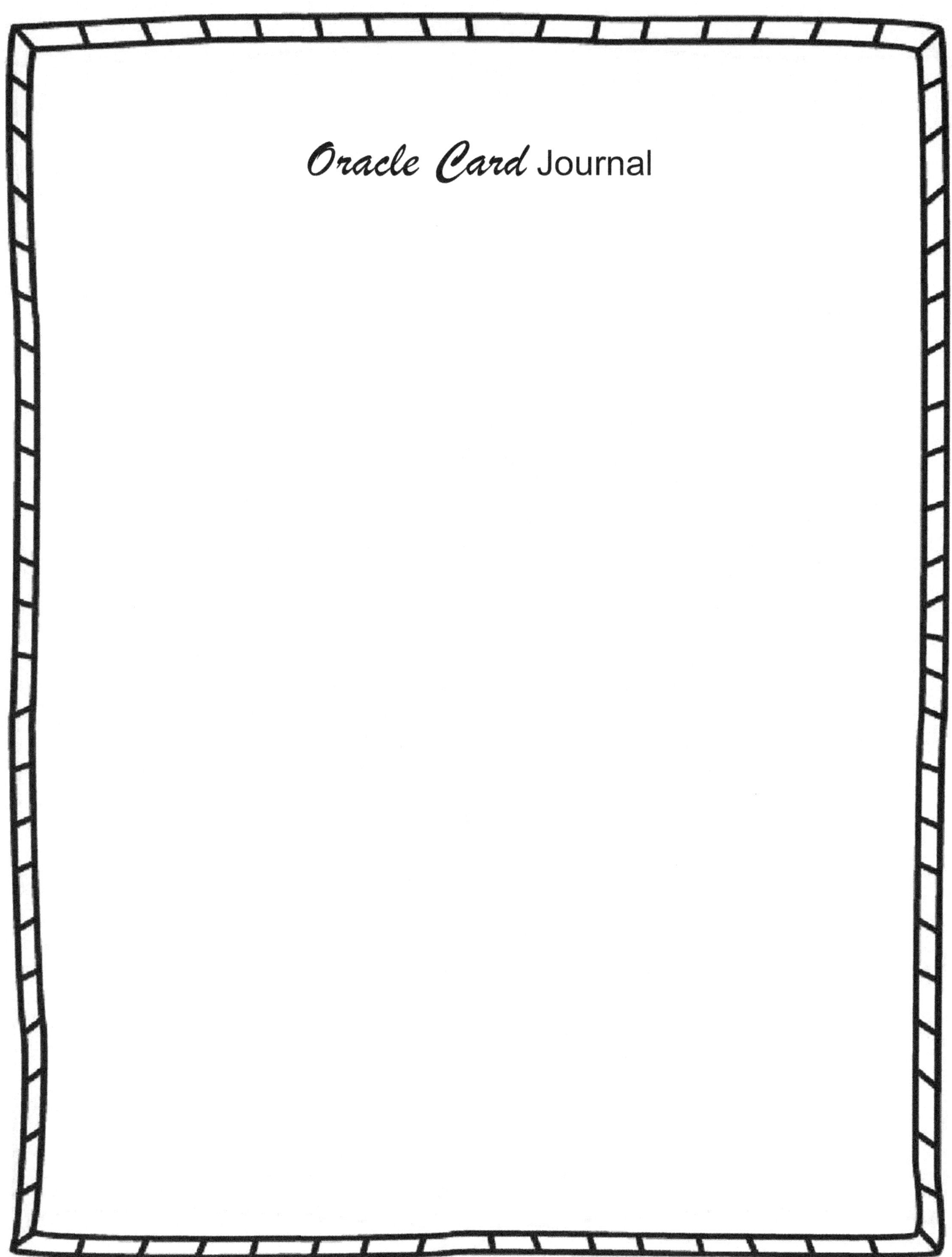

Oracle Card Journal

Intuitive *Chakra* Coloring

This exercise invites your intuition to lead the way. In fact, you will be coloring with your eyes closed, so your complete trust in what is happening is key to the magic of this exercise! This process also invites our chakras to communicate to us for personal guidance.

Our chakras are seven energetic centers that exist in our aura from the base of our spine to above our head. Each chakra (Sanskrit for 'disk') has a name and its own color. When looked at together, they create a beautiful rainbow within our energy field. Most importantly, each chakra has a special function that supports our overall health. I recommend doing your own research for a deeper understanding of this ancient topic, but for the purposes of this process, the information here is all that you need to benefit from the exercise. Take a look at the diagram and charts on the following pages.

Chakra Location & Color

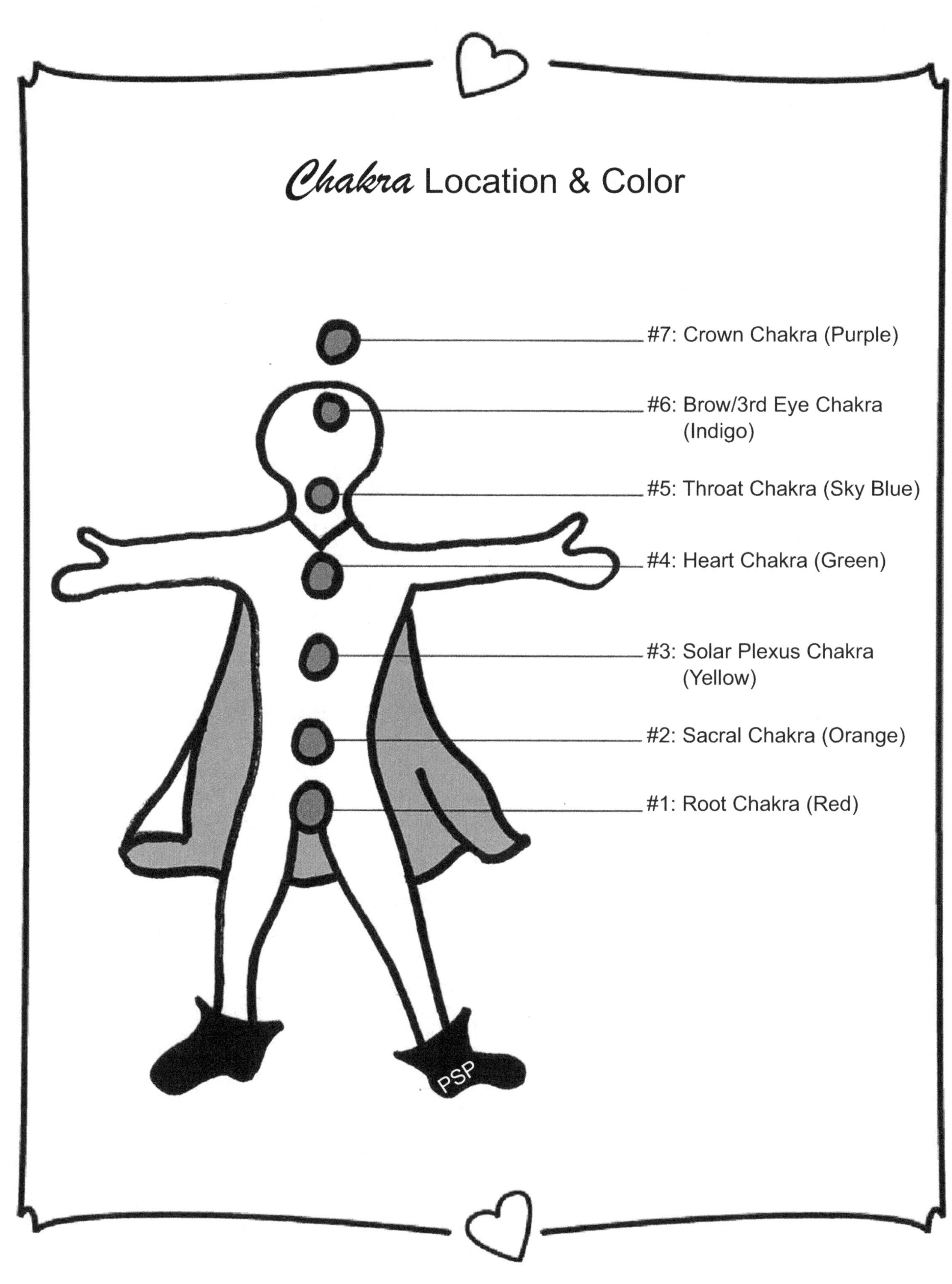

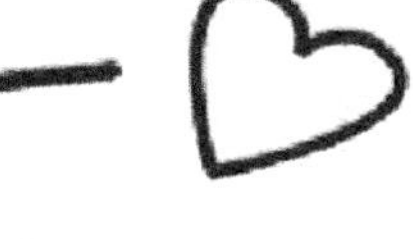

Chakra Chart

Read the chart below to understand the function and qualities of each chakra.

#1: ROOT CHAKRA (Red)

- Location: Base of spine · Themes: Survival, earth, grounding, matter, body, physical plane, home, family, roots, discipline, foundation, stillness
- Element: Earth · Right: To have
- Animals: Elephant, ox, bull
- Archetype: Earth Mother
- Foods: Proteins, meats

#2: SACRAL CHAKRA (Orange)

- Location: Lower ab/genitals
- Themes: Change, movement, polarity (opposites), desire, emotions, pleasure, sexuality, sensuality, intimacy, socializing, creativity
- Element: Water
- Right: To feel
- Animals: Fish, alligator
- Archetype: Eros
- Foods: Liquids

#3 SOLAR PLEXUS CHAKRA (Yellow)

- Location: Between naval and base of sternum
- Themes: Power, will, energy, metabolism, ease, humor, control, authority, aggression, warmth, transformation
- Element: Fire
- Right: To act
- Animals: Ram, lion
- Archetype: Magician, warrior
- Foods: Complex carbohydrates

#4 HEART CHAKRA (Green)

- Location: Center of the chest
- Themes: Balance, love, compassion, relationship, openness, giving, receiving, breath, affinity, grace, equilibrium, peace, forgiveness, harmony, group consciousness
- Element: Air
- Right: To love
- Animals: Antelope, dove
- Archetype: Aphrodite, Quan Yin, Christ
- Foods: Vegetables

Sources: The Sevenfold Journey by Anodea Judith & Selene Vega;
Chakra Awareness Guide - A.M.I.

Chakras Continued

<table>
<tr><td valign="top" width="50%">

#5: THROAT CHAKRA (Sky Blue)

- Location: Throat
- Themes: Vibration, rhythm, sound, harmony, connection, telepathy, communication, expression, creativity, singing/chanting, writing, public speaking, honesty
- Element: Ether · Right: To speak
- Animals: Elephant, bull
- Archetype: Hermes, Srasvati the Messenger
- Foods: Fruit

</td><td valign="top" width="50%">

#6: BROW/3RD EYE CHAKRA (Indigo)

- Location: Center of forehead
- Themes: Light/darkness, vision, beauty, dreams, memory, imagination, visualization, clairvoyance, intuition, concentration, peace of mind, wisdom, perception beyond duality
- Element: Light · Right: To see
- Animals: Owl, butterfly
- Archetype: Hermit, Psychic, Dreamer
- Foods: Consciousness-altering substances

</td></tr>
</table>

#7: CROWN CHAKRA (Violet)

- Location: Top of the head
- Themes: Consciousness, awareness, learning, intelligence, information, divinity, god/goddess, spirit, emptiness, the Infinite, selfless service
- Element: Thought
- Right: To know
- Animals: Elephant, ox, bull
- Archetype: Sage, Wisewoman, Shiva
- Foods: None. Fasting

Sources: The Sevenfold Journey by Anodea Judith & Selene Vega; Chakra Awareness Guide - A.M.I.

Intuitive *Chakra* Coloring

OBJECTIVE: To ask a question and create an intuitive drawing, with eyes closed, using the colors of the chakras. The answer to your question will be found in your drawing from the chakra colors, their meaning, and your drawing's marks, words, and images.

SUPPLIES: Seven crayons — each one corresponding to the individual chakra colors. You'll also need a bowl for the crayons, a timer, the chakra chart, blank drawing pages, and journal page in the workbook.

INSTRUCTIONS:

1. Identify your heart's three questions. Example: How can I be of service to the world?

2. With <u>eyes closed</u>, select one crayon. Open your eyes and write your first question across the top of the first page. Do this two more times—one crayon and one page per question.

3. Choose one page/question to create your first intuitive drawing/coloring.

4. Set your timer for forty-five seconds. Place your bowl of crayons close within reach.

5. Start the timer and begin drawing with <u>eyes closed</u>. Select crayons intuitively with <u>eyes closed</u>.

6. Allow your intuition to guide you. Scribbling is allowed! If you wish to sketch or write, honor those impulses. Select new colors whenever you wish. All with <u>eyes closed</u>.

7. Stop when you hear the alarm, and open your eyes.

8. Process your drawing using the journal page.

9. After you become comfortable with the process, add other colored crayons. Before you use them, take a moment to determine each color's symbolic meaning. This way you will understand its guidance when it appears in a drawing. For example, black might mean surrender—gold might mean spirituality—and turquoise might mean freedom. You decide!

Drawing #1:

My Question: ____

Drawing #2:

My Question: _______________________________________

Drawing #3:

My Question: ____

Chakra Drawing Journal

(use for each drawing)

1. What initial feelings emerge when you gaze at your whole picture?

2. What is the meaning of the various chakra colors in your drawing?

3. What is the meaning of your various marks, words, and images?

4. How do images relate to others (do images overlap or connect with others?)

5. What is the relationship between the images and colors?

6. What is the meaning of the color with which you wrote your question?

7. Which predominant chakras are speaking to you now?

8. What guidance is surfacing from your drawing?

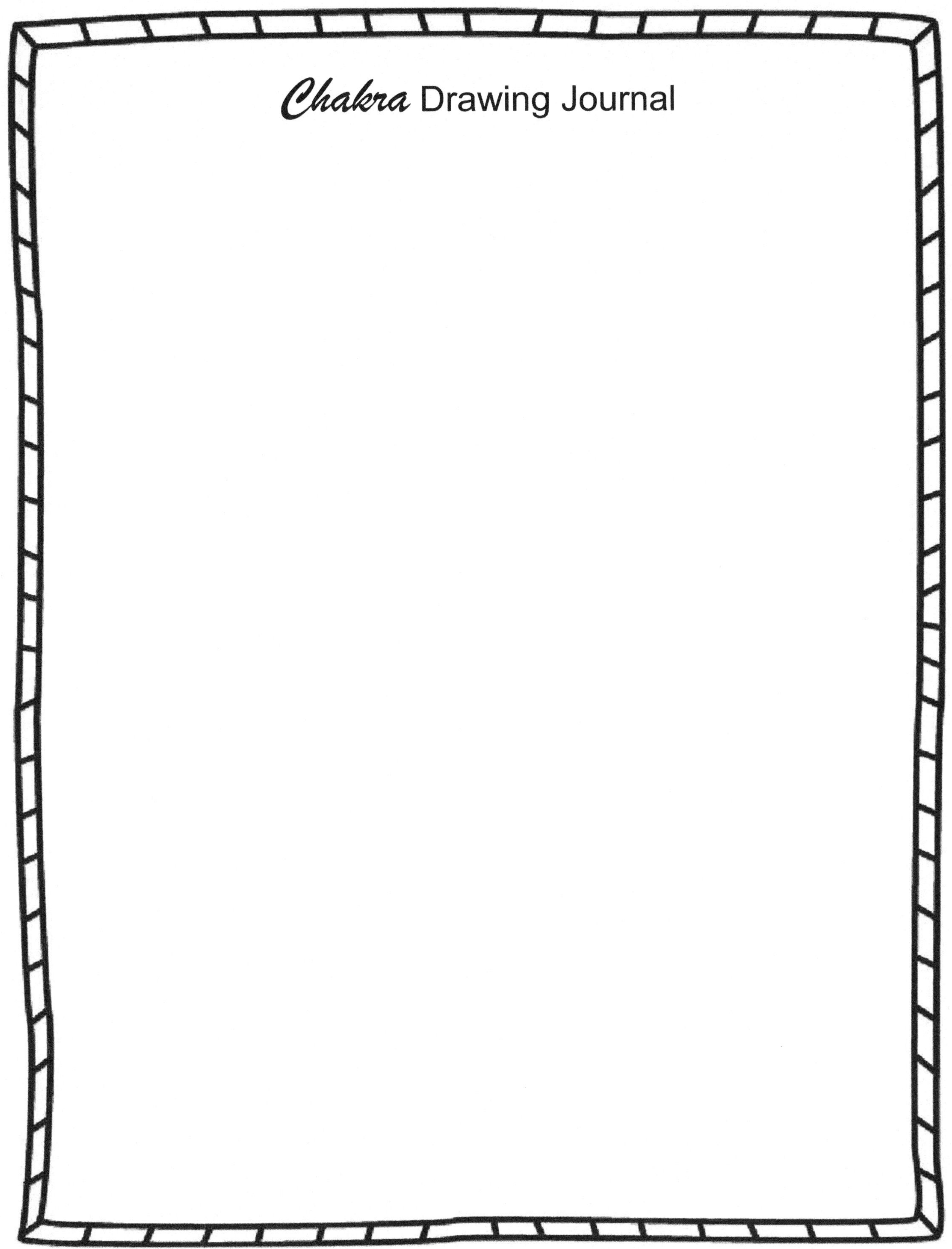

Chakra Drawing Journal

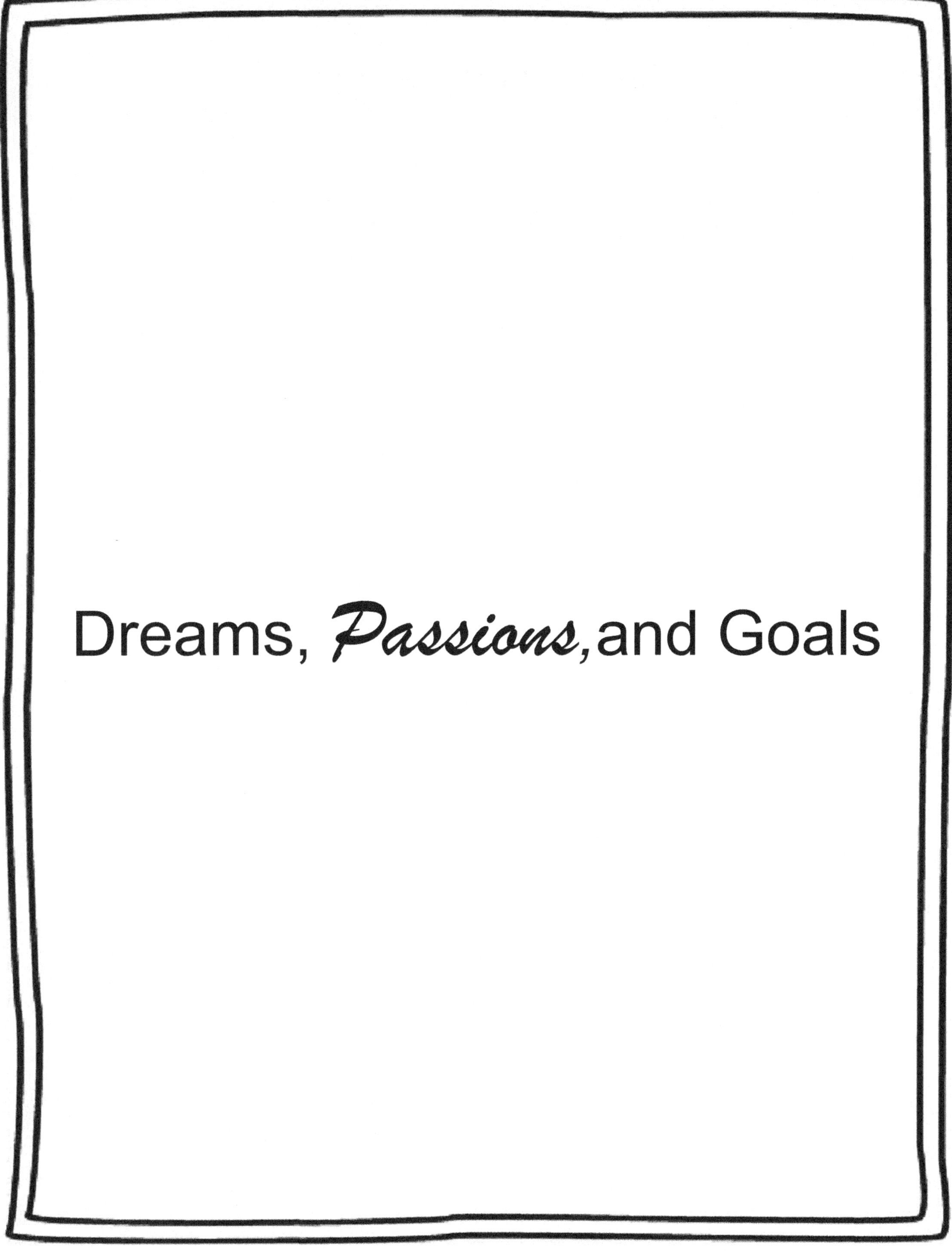

Dreams, *Passions,* and Goals

Draw Your *'Soul-ogo'*

Refer back to your three Soul Powers or select three new ones. Imagine how these three powers would somehow blend. Draw and color one logo (or 'soul-ogo') that represents the combined power of this trio. This is your soul's current logo! Business logos often change as the company changes, so you may re-do your logo from time to time as your interests change.

Write Your *'Soul-ogan'*

Next, create a slogan (or 'soul-ogan') to accompany your 'soul-logo'! Slogans are concise and meaningful phrases used to advertise a business or product. Nike's famous "Just Do It" slogan is an example. Slogans speak to the heart of the product or service. Your 'soul-ogan' will enhance your 'soul-ogo'! Write a few versions and then tune into which one best expresses your heart and soul today.

Personal *Myth*

I love the <u>The Wizard of Oz</u>. I mean, who can't relate to Dorothy wanting to go over the rainbow in search of her heart's desires? The fact that so many of us can relate to her adventure is because of the power behind the hero's myth. They are written to reflect the human experience.

The hero's myth is an adventure story in which the main character leaves home, faces a set of challenges, and then returns home significantly changed in some way. We ourselves do this again and again throughout our lives, literally and metaphorically. Joseph Campbell (1904-1987) taught us that our lives are mythical in structure, and, like Dorothy and Odysseus, we are the heroes. Campbell, too, coined the phrase, "follow your bliss," which is exactly what the hero sets off to do in the first place. They are heeding the call of their inner desires. And since myth contains elements of fantasy and magic, anything can happen along the way! So, the adventure is sure to be an epic one.

During this process, you will connect with your own, personal myth that reflects a current goal or dream. This section has multiple steps, and you are encouraged to move at your own pace.

You will begin with a writing exercise, followed by an intuitive drawing and a myth writing exercise. All of this can then be processed through the journal prompts. The myth writing portion of this process was first shared with me by author, coach, and dear friend, Susyn Reeve of susynreeve.com.

This exercise is a big invitation to surrender and allow whatever wishes to emerge from within you to do so. Allow your intuition and heart to guide the way. And have fun!

Personal *Myth:* What's Calling You Now?

(a dream, desire, or curiosity)

This is an intuitive writing exercise. First, set a timer for five minutes. After you hit start, write, write, write in response to the above question. Stop when five minutes has ended.

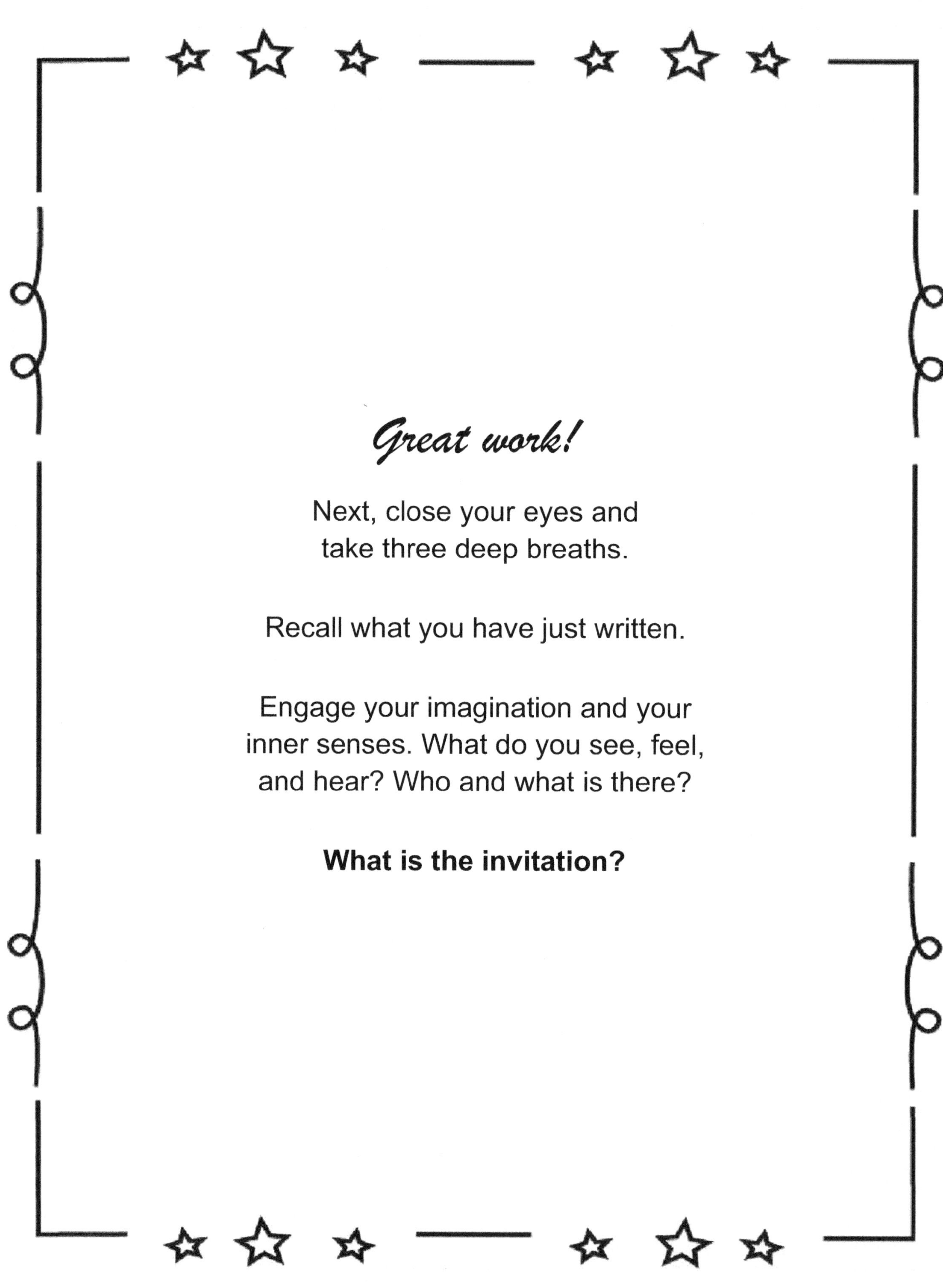

Great work!

Next, close your eyes and
take three deep breaths.

Recall what you have just written.

Engage your imagination and your
inner senses. What do you see, feel,
and hear? Who and what is there?

What is the invitation?

Personal *Myth* Drawing

Draw and color what you noticed and felt as you reflected on
what you wrote. Your drawing can be as literal or as abstract as you wish.

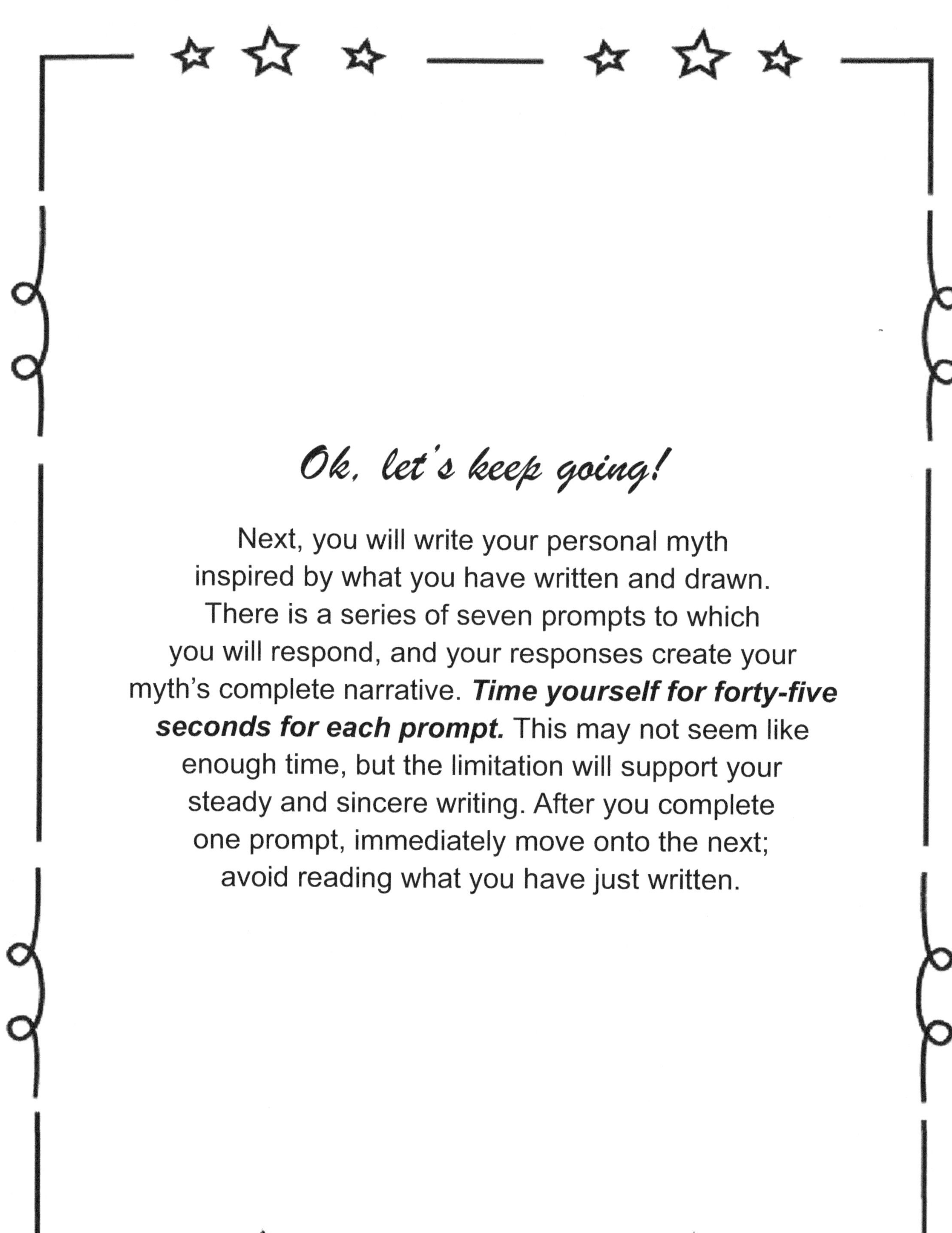

Ok, let's keep going!

Next, you will write your personal myth
inspired by what you have written and drawn.
There is a series of seven prompts to which
you will respond, and your responses create your
myth's complete narrative. **Time yourself for forty-five
seconds for each prompt.** This may not seem like
enough time, but the limitation will support your
steady and sincere writing. After you complete
one prompt, immediately move onto the next;
avoid reading what you have just written.

Myth Prompt 1: Once upon a time…

Myth Prompt 2: Everyday...

Myth Prompt 3: Until one day…

Myth Prompt 4: And because of this...

Myth Prompt 5: And because of this…

Myth Prompt 6: Until finally...

Myth Prompt 7: And ever since that day…

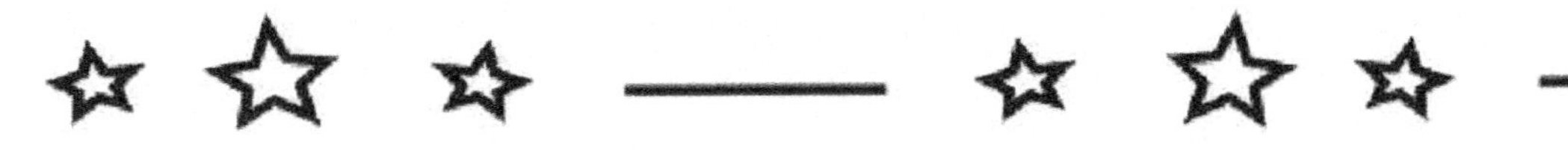

Personal *Myth* Journal

1. In your myth, what gifts are you sharing?

2. What challenges do you face? What support do you need to overcome these?

3. What are you releasing? What would you like in place of what is released?

4. What beliefs support your myth?

5. What is the title of your myth?

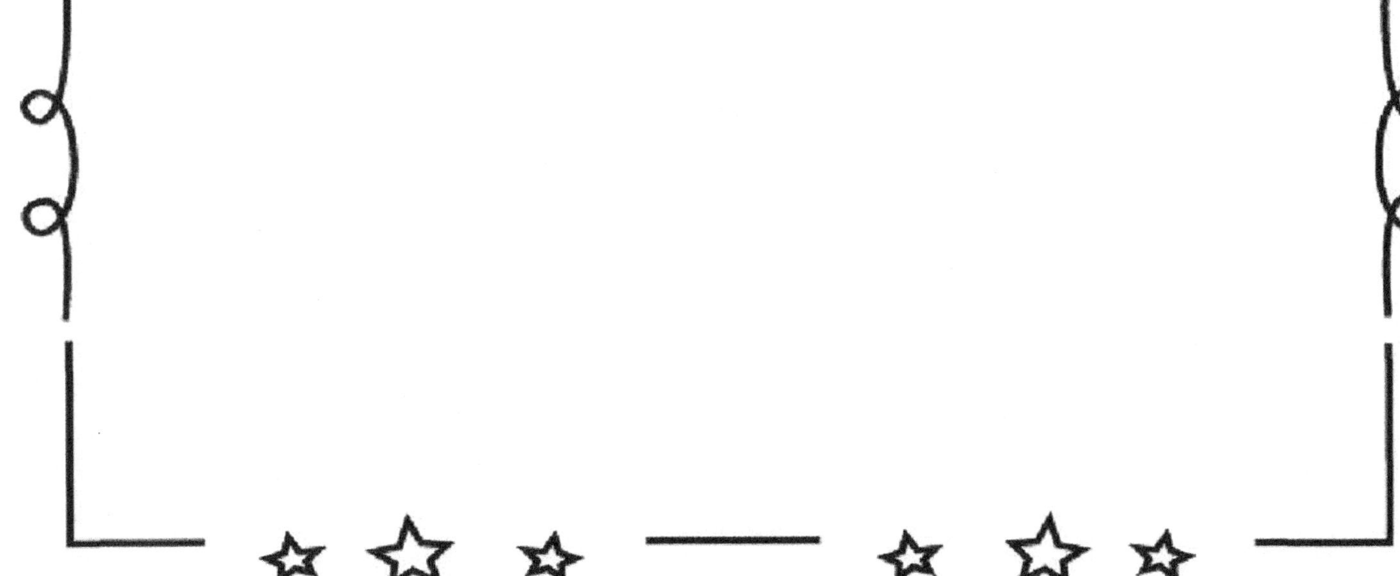

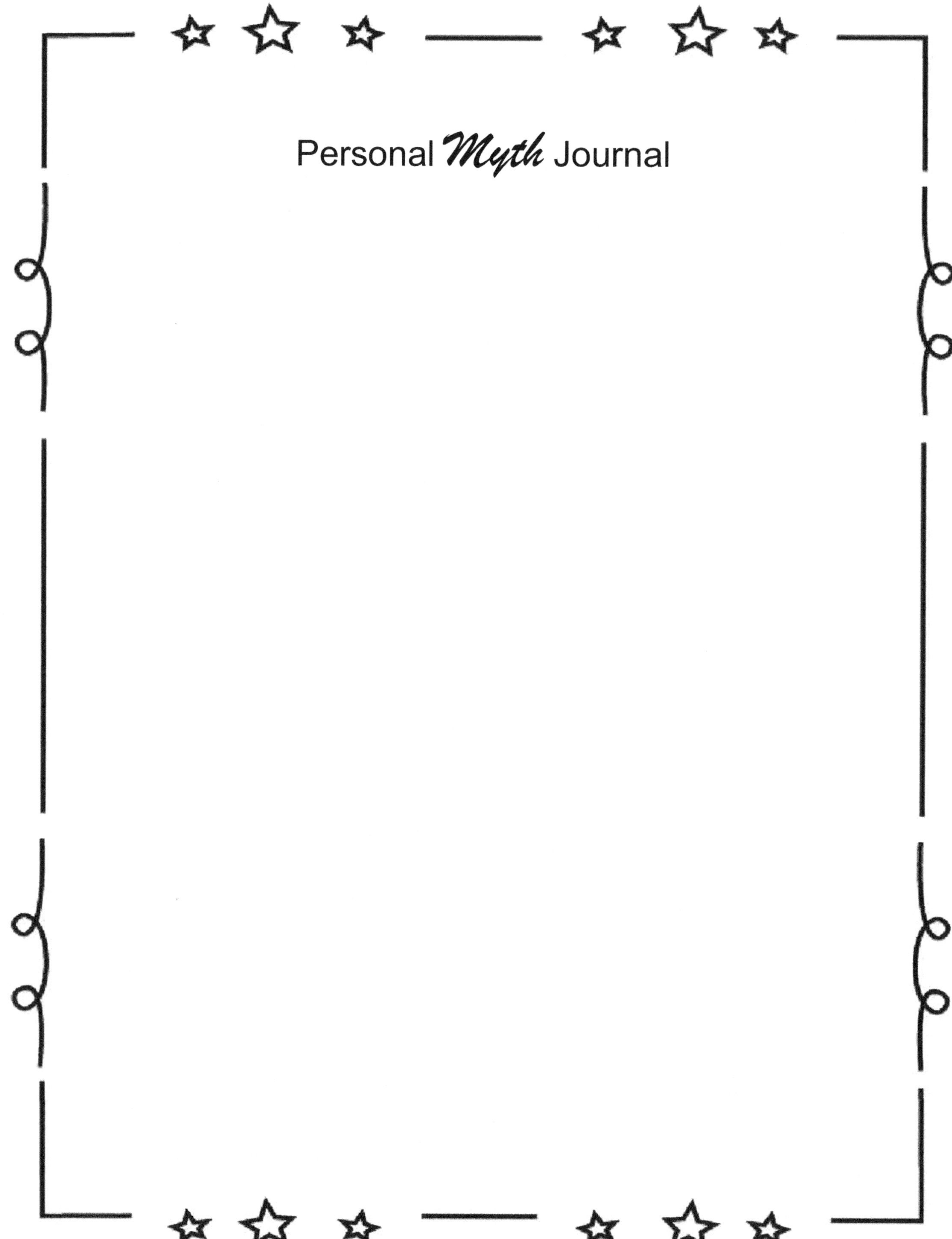# Personal *Myth* Journal

Come Out Everyday

In the fall of 1998, as a young freshman in college, I 'came out of the closet' to finally embrace and announce my homosexuality. The phrase 'coming out' is usually applied to anyone on the LGBTQ+ spectrum when they are in the same process. I believe, however, that we all—regardless of our sexual orientation—can come out of the closet everyday about anything that we personally wish to accept about ourselves and proclaim to the world!

Coming out requires courage and faith. It is a radical act! My coming out made me realize that I can survive hard things and that I wasn't an outcast, which I had feared I would become. It was a rebirth from a sort of death that I survived. When we come out we defy all odds, fears, and what others (and ourselves) deem as abnormal, impossible, or even bad. And therefore we become super human!

What do you wish to embrace and share now with yourself, one person, or the world? A new passion? An emotional truth? An unpopular interest? How would you like to come out of your closet?

For this process, you'll begin with a free write exercise followed by an intuitive drawing. The process will conclude with the journal questions.

Here are some suggestions:

- Take a deep breath before you begin. Know that you are safe in this process. You do not need to share what you write and draw with anyone if you do not want to.

- Play music that emboldens you to imagine your coming out! My favorite song for this occasion? Well, that would be Diana Ross's "I'm Coming Out." Obviously!

Come Out Everyday:

How Do You Wish to Come Out?

This is an intuitive writing exercise. First, set a timer for five minutes. After you hit start, write, write, write in response to the above question. Stop when five minutes has ended.

Come Out Everyday Drawing

Draw and color yourself coming out of the closet as you embrace and share your new truth. Include at least one ally whom you trust to support your coming out process.

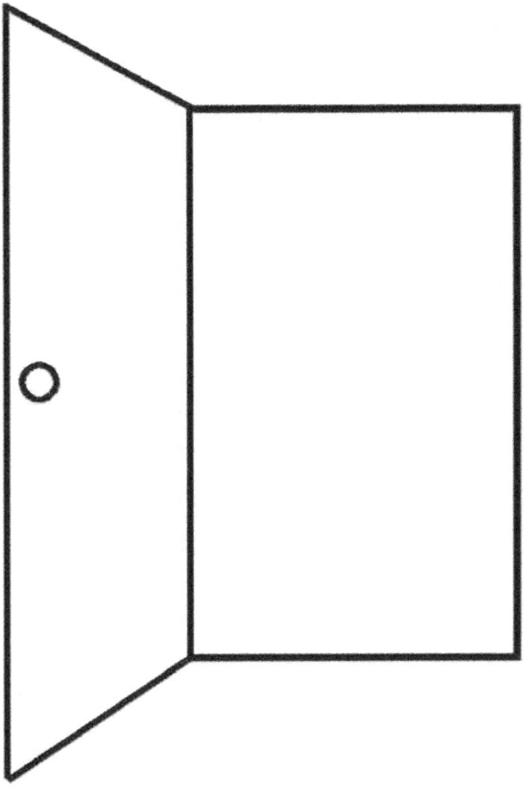

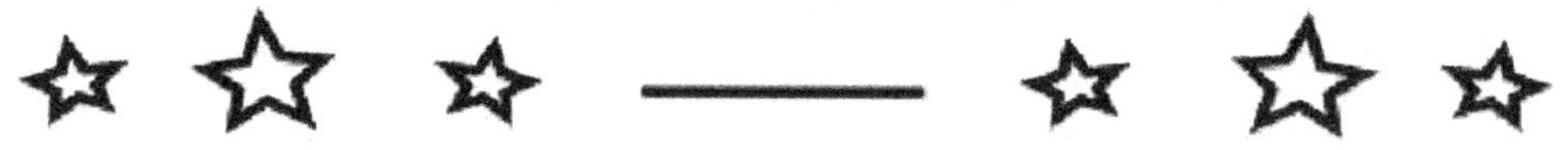

Come Out Journal

1. What is happening NOW in your coming out process?

2. How can you move through with ease and grace?

3. What are you learning through this cycle in life?

4. What is currently leaving your life as you come out?

5. What is currently coming into your life?

6. What is your medicine (healing support) for the moment?

7. Who or what is your ally? How can they provide support for you now?

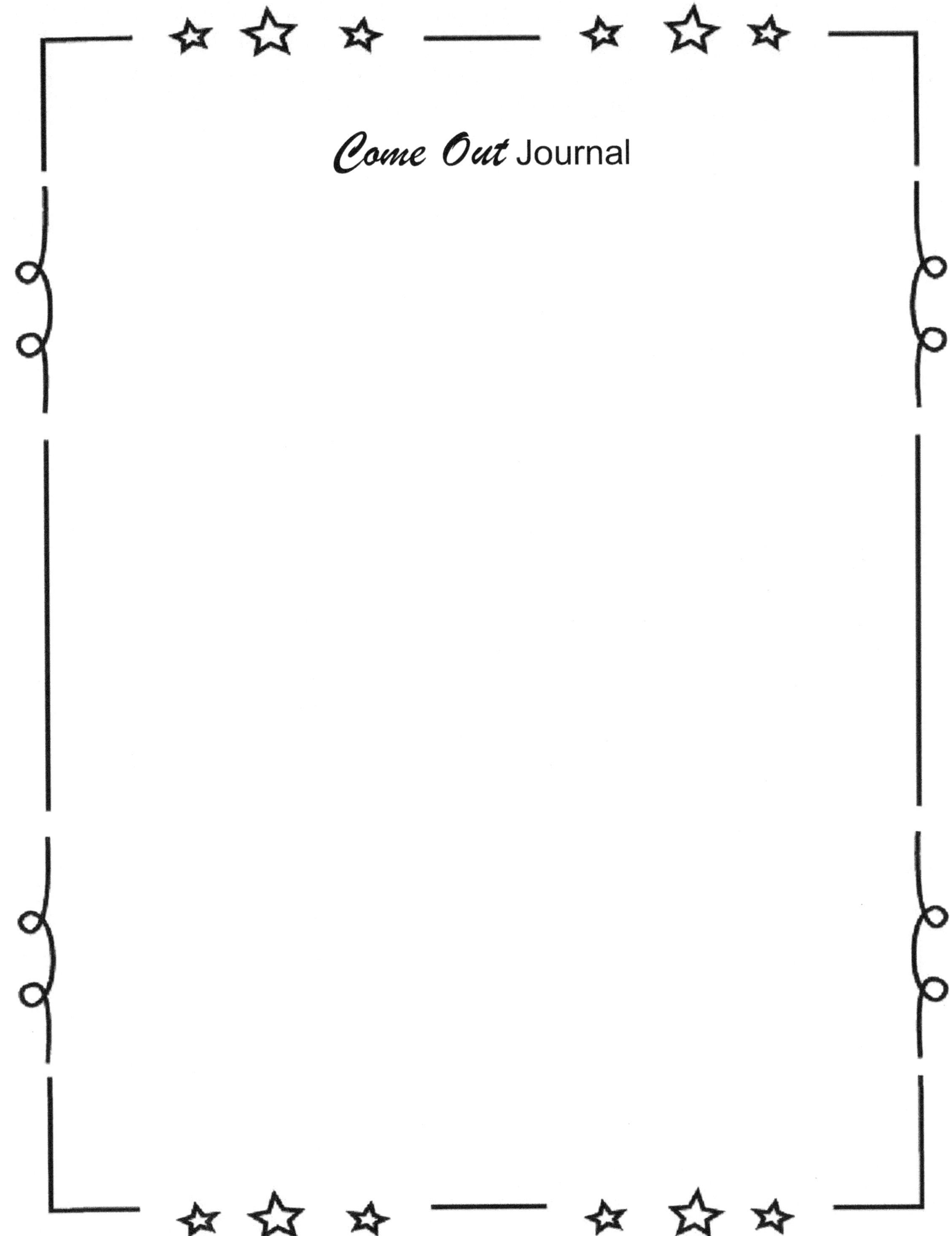

Come Out Journal

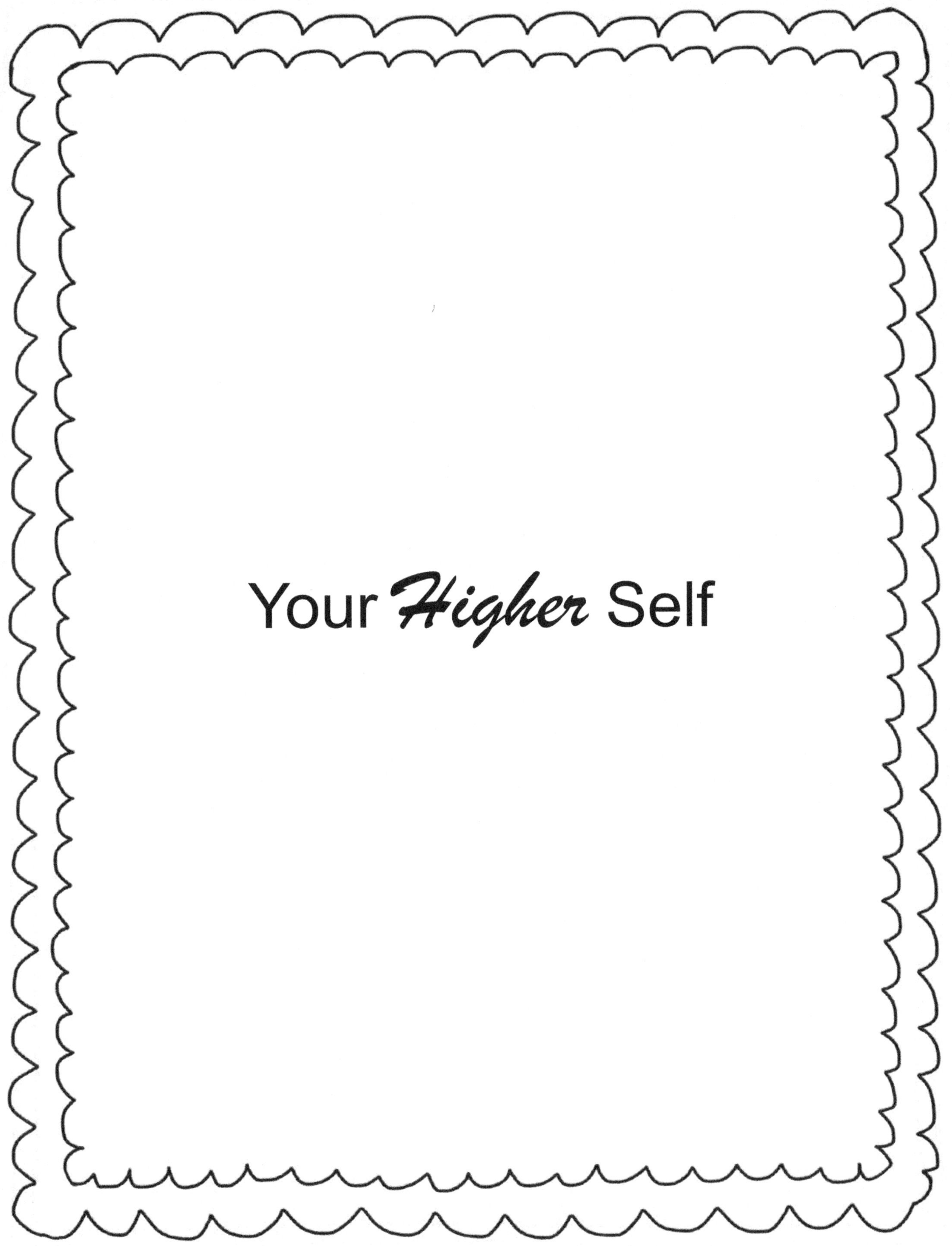

Your *Higher* Self

Out of the *Rainbow*

For this process, you will begin with a visualization and then create an intuitive drawing of what you experienced. This is an invitation to engage all the resources of your imagination and to ALLOW whatever wishes to emerge from within you to do so.

Consider recording the script on the next page using an electronic device so that you can listen to it and relax fully during the meditation. You may also do this exercise with a friend who can read the script to you. However you decide to do this, be sure to read slowly with frequent pauses to allow your imagination time to do its job. When you're ready to begin, find a comfortable place to sit or lie down. Close your eyes, and take three deep breaths. Then begin the visualization.

Rainbow Visualization:

Imagine that you are in your favorite outdoor setting. This is your choice. If more than one outdoor setting comes to mind, simply choose one setting for now.

You feel calm, safe, and at peace here. See what there is to see...hear what there is to hear...smell what there is to smell...taste what there is to taste...and feel what there is to feel, physically and emotionally. Breathe in the fresh air. Breathe deeply. Take a few moments in silence to enjoy this relaxing place. When you're ready, find a place to sit or lie down.

As you gaze upward, you see a rainbow forming in the sky. The rainbow becomes larger, more pronounced, and saturated. It is an ideal rainbow, and you feel a sense of peace and calm as you observe it. Next, you notice a ball of bright white light forming and growing in the center of the colorful rainbow. As you observe this soft, warm light, you feel safe and at peace. You next sense movement within the light, and then, from out of the light, in the center of the multi-colored rainbow, a benevolent being emerges. You have never seen this being before, and it is no one that you know. The loving being gently descends to the ground where you can observe its detailed appearance and features.

How do they appear? What is the being wearing? What colors do you notice? Are they female, male, or other? How old do they seem? Are they human-like or from another realm? How does their face appear to you? Are they holding or carrying anything special? How do you feel in their presence?

The being wishes to present you with a gift. Would you like to receive it? If so, extend your hands and receive the gift. What is it? Is it literal or symbolic in meaning? Quietly to yourself, express gratitude for the gift. The being then gently ascends back up into the white light within the center of the rainbow. You gaze up, feeling an even deeper sense of peace, calm, and gratitude.

Now, take a long deep breath. Slowly begin to wiggle and shift your body, and, in your own time, return to the room and present time by gently opening your eyes.

Out of the *Rainbow*

Draw and color the being from the rainbow. Include the gift that you received.

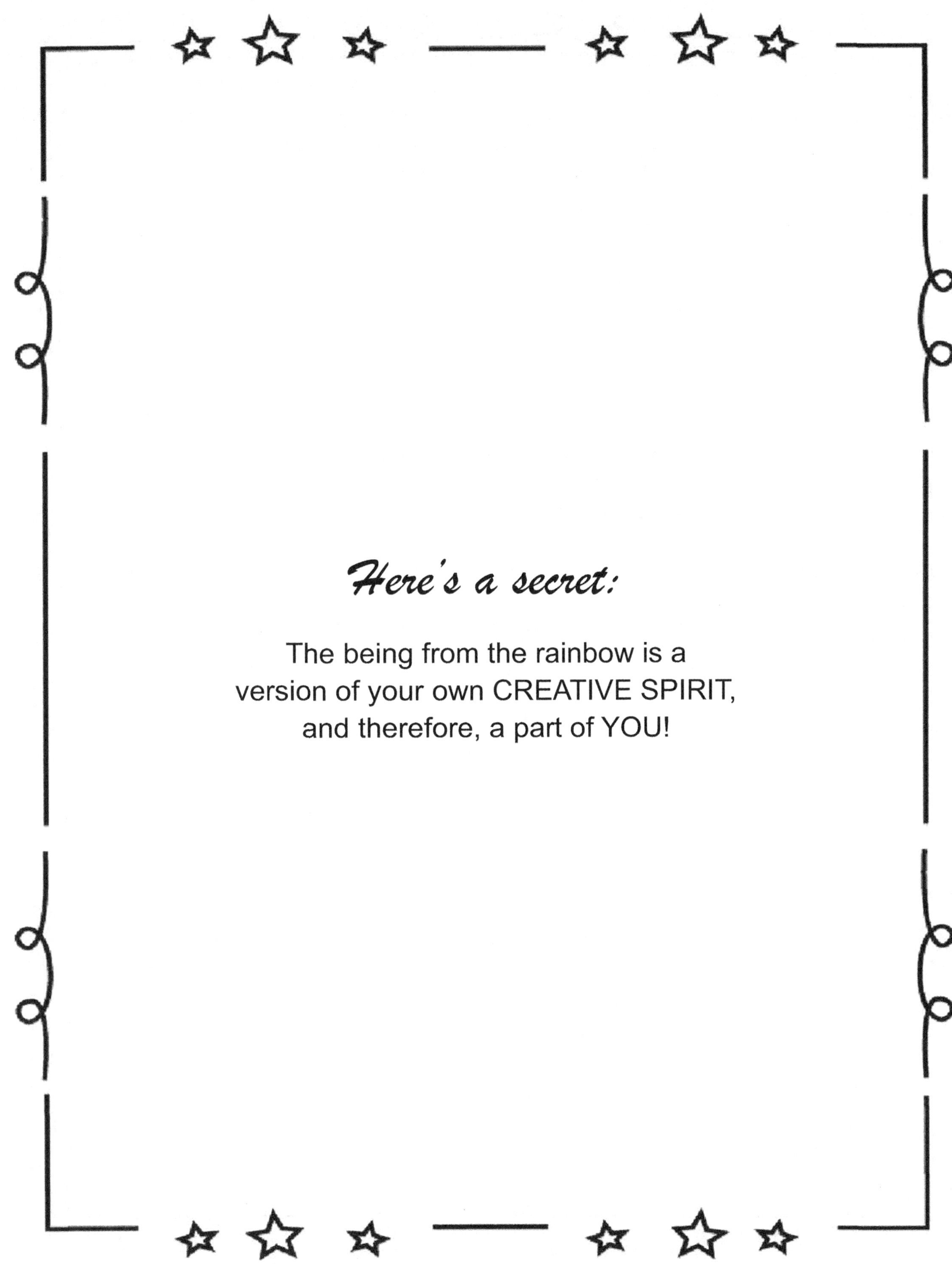

Here's a secret:

The being from the rainbow is a
version of your own CREATIVE SPIRIT,
and therefore, a part of YOU!

Creative Spirit Journal

1. What are five words that describe your creative spirit?

2. How do you relate with your creative spirit and what is most appealing about them?

3. How do your creative spirit's traits and abilities show up in your life and practices? When do you feel most aligned with your creative spirit?

4. What does your creative spirit need in order to thrive?

5. Does your creative spirit have a name?

6. What is your creative spirit's relationship with fear?

7. What radical acts does your creative spirit enjoy performing?

8. What is the significance of the gift that you received? How would you like to honor the gift in the coming days?

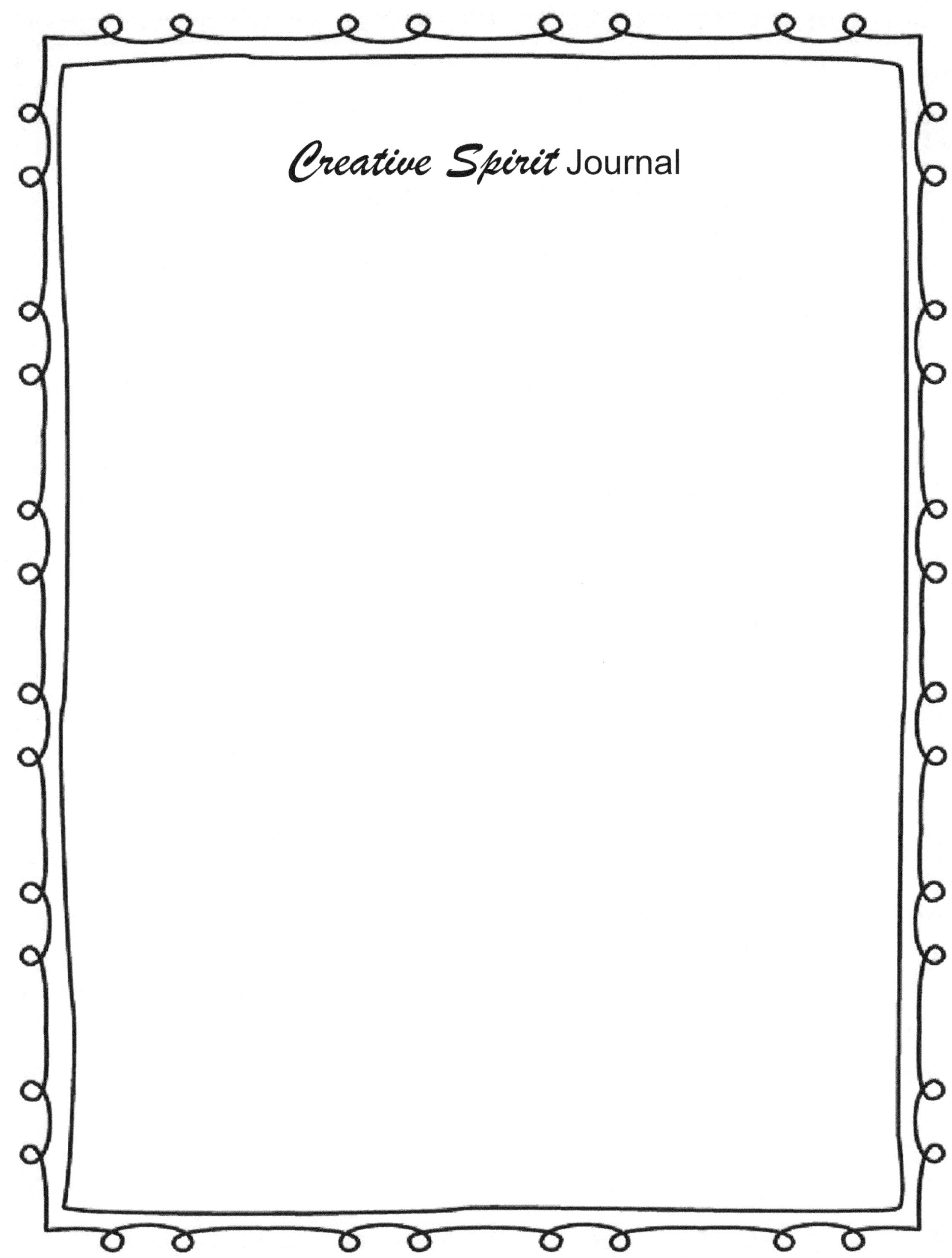
Creative Spirit Journal

Your Sacred *Duality*

I believe we are comprised of balanced light and shadow at all times. This is what I call our sacred duality. While we may not wish to possess the uncomfortable shadow aspects of ourselves (what we fear and criticize), the truth of the matter is that our lives ultimately benefit from these lessons. And, as they say, our genius lies within our shadow. Our most radical and liberating reform can be born from the shadows, and our wrestling with them can ultimately resolve with our re-connection to love, self-acceptance, and peace.

This is an advanced exercise for those interested in exploring their sacred duality. It has multiple stages and requires more time than other exercises. You will begin each step with a visualization and then create intuitive drawings of what you experienced during the visualization. Each stage concludes with in-depth processing. Overall, this is an invitation to engage all the resources of your imagination and to ALLOW whatever wishes to emerge from within you to do so .

Consider recording the visualization scripts using an electronic device so that you can listen to them and relax fully during the meditations. You may also do this exercise with a friend who can read the scripts to you. When you're ready to begin the visualizations, find a comfortable place to sit or lie down. Close your eyes, and take a few deep breaths. Then begin.

Here are some suggestions:

- Don't look ahead in this section! The magic of this process comes from the element of surprise.

- Take your time as you work through this process. You do not need to complete this exercise in one sitting.

- Whether you record the scripts or have a friend read them to you, be sure to read them slowly with frequent pauses in order to allow your imagination time to do its job.

Sacred *Duality* Visualization #1

Imagine that you are in your favorite outdoor setting. This is your choice. If more than one outdoor setting comes to mind, simply choose one setting for now.

You feel calm, safe, and at peace here. See what there is to see...hear what there is to hear...smell what there is to smell...taste what there is to taste...and feel what there is to feel, physically and emotionally. Breathe in the fresh air. Breathe deeply. Take a few moments in silence to enjoy this relaxing place. When you're ready, find a place to sit down.

You gaze ahead and notice a long, smooth path. It extends as far as your eyes can see. Next, you notice that someone is on the path, far ahead, moving towards you. As you observe this, you feel a sense of inner calm and peace. You know that this being is a good friend; in fact, they are your ideal mentor.

You have never seen this being before, and it is no one that you know. Your ideal mentor is the being whom you regard as the perfect guide and teacher for your unique and creative life.

Your ideal mentor gets closer and eventually pauses before you. You are able to observe their appearance in more detail. How do they appear? What are they wearing? What colors do you notice? Are they female, male, or other? How old do they seem? Are they human-like or from another realm? How does their face appear to you? Are they holding or carrying anything special? How do you feel in their presence? Finally, tune in to how your mentor supports you.

Quietly to yourself, express gratitude for this special visit. Your ideal mentor then turns and begins walking away along the path. You watch them leave feeling a deep sense of peace, calm, and gratitude.

Now, take a long deep breath. Slowly begin to wiggle and shift your body, and, in your own time, return to the room and present time by gently opening your eyes.

Sacred *Duality:*

Draw and Color Your Ideal Mentor

Sacred *Duality* Visualization #2

Imagine that you are walking down the sidewalk of a crowded and noisy city. Next, imagine yourself enveloped in an invisible protective bubble. Inside you are perfectly safe from any harm, and you can see clearly and breathe fully and easily.

You notice people everywhere as they rush by you. You can hear the city's cacophonous sounds, and you can smell pollutants in the air. You can see the hazy smog in the air, covering the sky and partially blocking the light. The tall gray skyscrapers loom all around you, as hundreds of cars, buses, and trucks speed by down the congested streets.

As you turn the corner you look across the street and notice a peculiar being casually looking back at you. This is your ideal nemesis—the most challenging being that you could ever encounter. They trigger your most difficult feelings. You have never seen this being before, and it is no one that you know. Now, take a few deep breaths. Remember that you are perfectly safe within your protective bubble. You can breathe deeply and safely observe your ideal nemesis from a distance. If you'd like you may also call upon your ideal mentor, creative spirit, or a guardian angel to be by your side as you safely observe your ideal nemesis.

From where you stand, you are able to observe their appearance in detail. How do they appear? What are they wearing? What colors do you notice? Are they female, male, or other? How old do they seem? Are they human-like or from another realm? How does their face appear to you? Are they holding or carrying anything special? How do you feel in their presence? Finally, tune in to how specifically your ideal nemesis challenges you.

Now, take a long deep breath and exhale. As you exhale, you notice that your ideal nemesis begins to easily disappear, like vapor into the air. Continue to breathe and exhale, gently, until it has completely gone. Shift your awareness back to your own room. See your room in your mind's eye. You are here now and very safe. Slowly begin to wiggle and shift your body, and in your own time, return to the room and present moment by gently opening your eyes.

Sacred *Duality:*

Draw and Color Your Ideal Nemesis

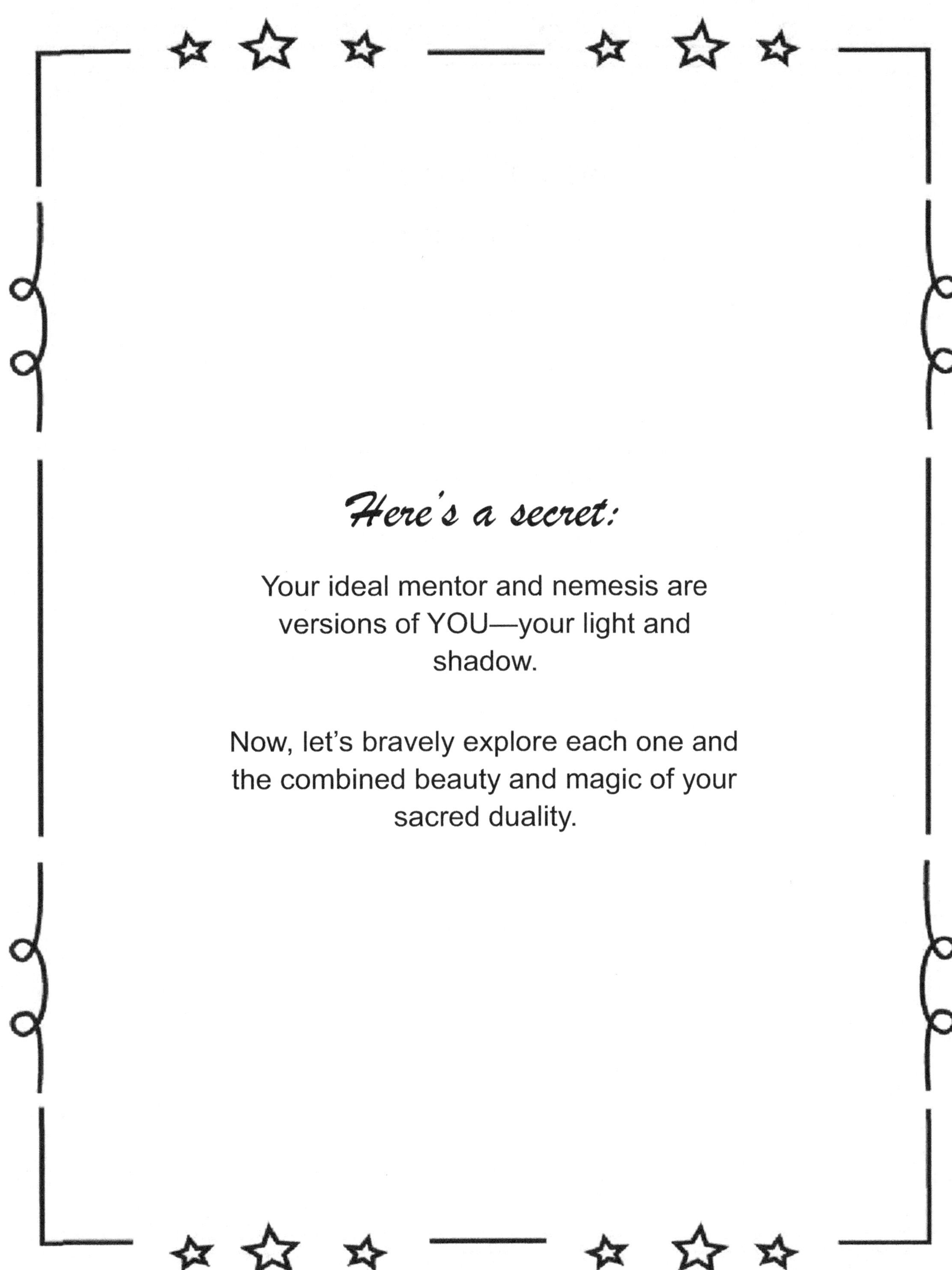

Here's a secret:

Your ideal mentor and nemesis are versions of YOU—your light and shadow.

Now, let's bravely explore each one and the combined beauty and magic of your sacred duality.

Sacred *Duality:*

Ideal Mentor Journal

1.   What are five words that describe your ideal mentor?

2.   How do you relate with your ideal mentor and what is most appealing about them?

3.   How do your ideal mentor's traits and abilities show up in your life and practices? When do you feel most aligned with your ideal mentor?

4.   What does your ideal mentor need in order to thrive?

5.   Does your ideal mentor have a name?

6.   What radical acts does your ideal mentor enjoy performing?

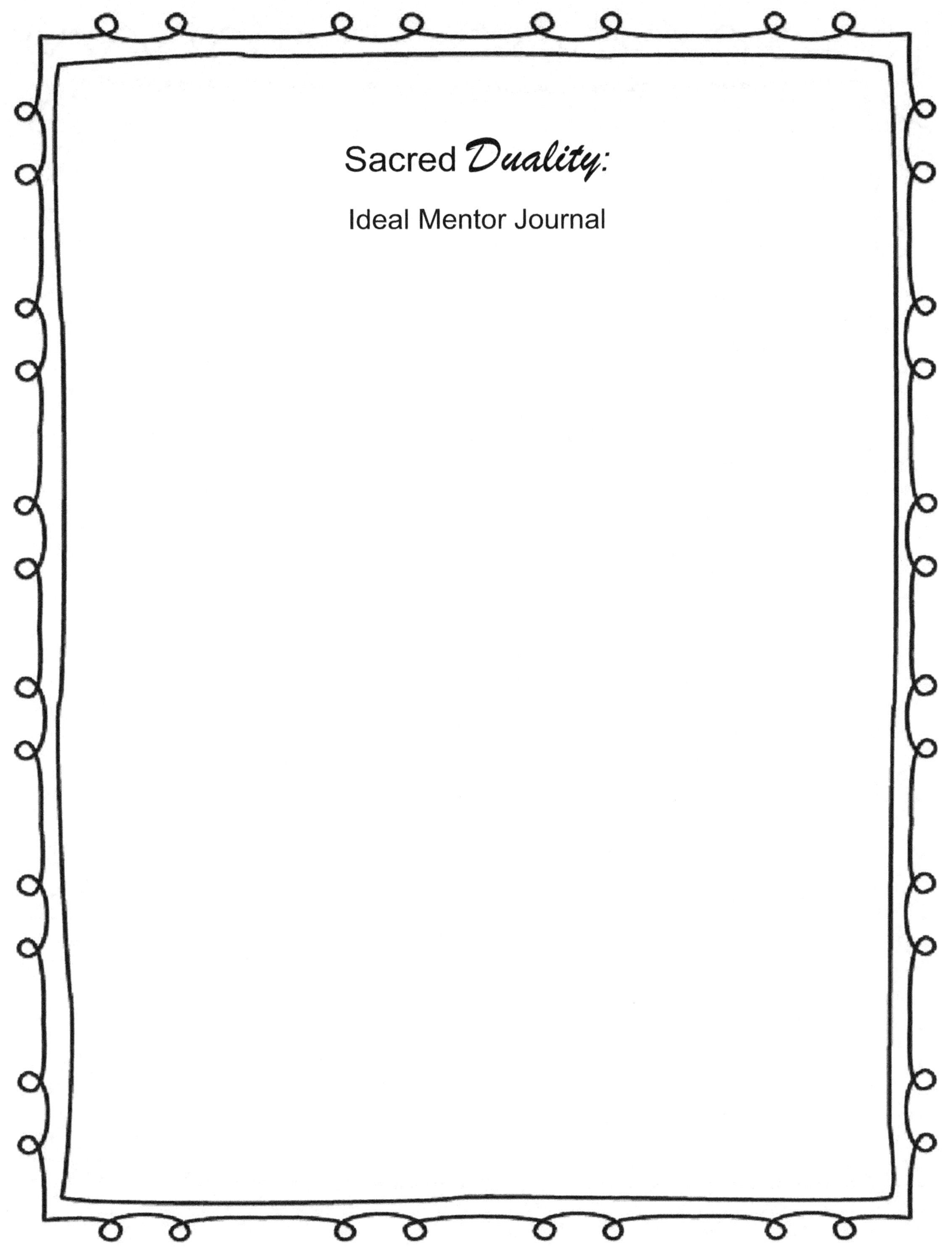

Sacred *Duality:*

Ideal Mentor Journal

Sacred *Duality:*

Ideal Nemesis Journal

1. What are five words that describe your nemesis?

2. How do you feel towards your nemesis? When do you feel that way about yourself or others?

3. When do your nemesis's traits and behaviors show up in your life and actices?

4. What positive behavior would occur if your nemesis channeled one of its traits/behaviors with a loving intention? For example, a judgmental person could become a successful art critic or a physically reckless person could become a fierce dancer.

5. What are the loveable needs beneath each of your nemesis's fearful traits/behaviors? How can you honor these needs?

6. Where are there opportunities for forgiveness? Between yourself and your nemesis? Between your mentor and nemesis? Are YOU willing to forgive YOURSELF?

7. Does your ideal nemesis have a name?

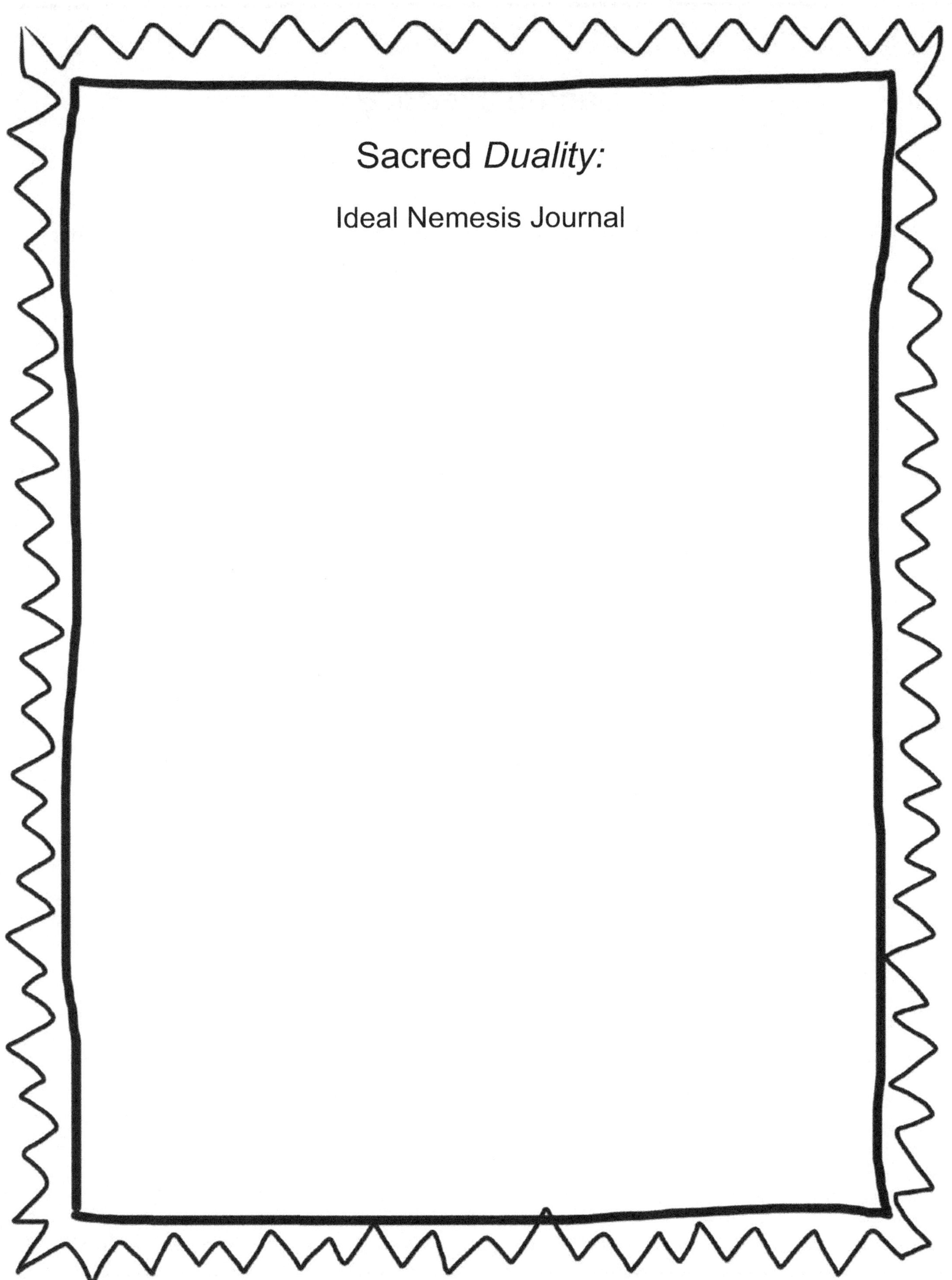

Sacred *Duality:*

Ideal Nemesis Journal

Sacred *Duality:*

Draw and Color Your Blended Self

You've met your mentor and nemesis—your yin and yang. Let's now imagine them as one, divinely united in a sacred, creative, and positive way. Close your eyes. Using all the resources of your imagination, call in your mentor and then call in your nemesis. Invite them to merge into one being. As they blend together what do you notice? How does your blended self look and feel?

Sacred *Duality:*

Blended Self Journal

1. What are five words that describe your blended self?

2. How do you feel in the presence of your blended self?

3. How do you relate with your blended self, and what is most appealing about them?

4. How do your blended self's traits and abilities show up in your life and practices? Where is there room for more?

5. What does your blended self need in order to thrive?

6. What radical acts does your blended self enjoy performing?

7. Does your blended self have a name?

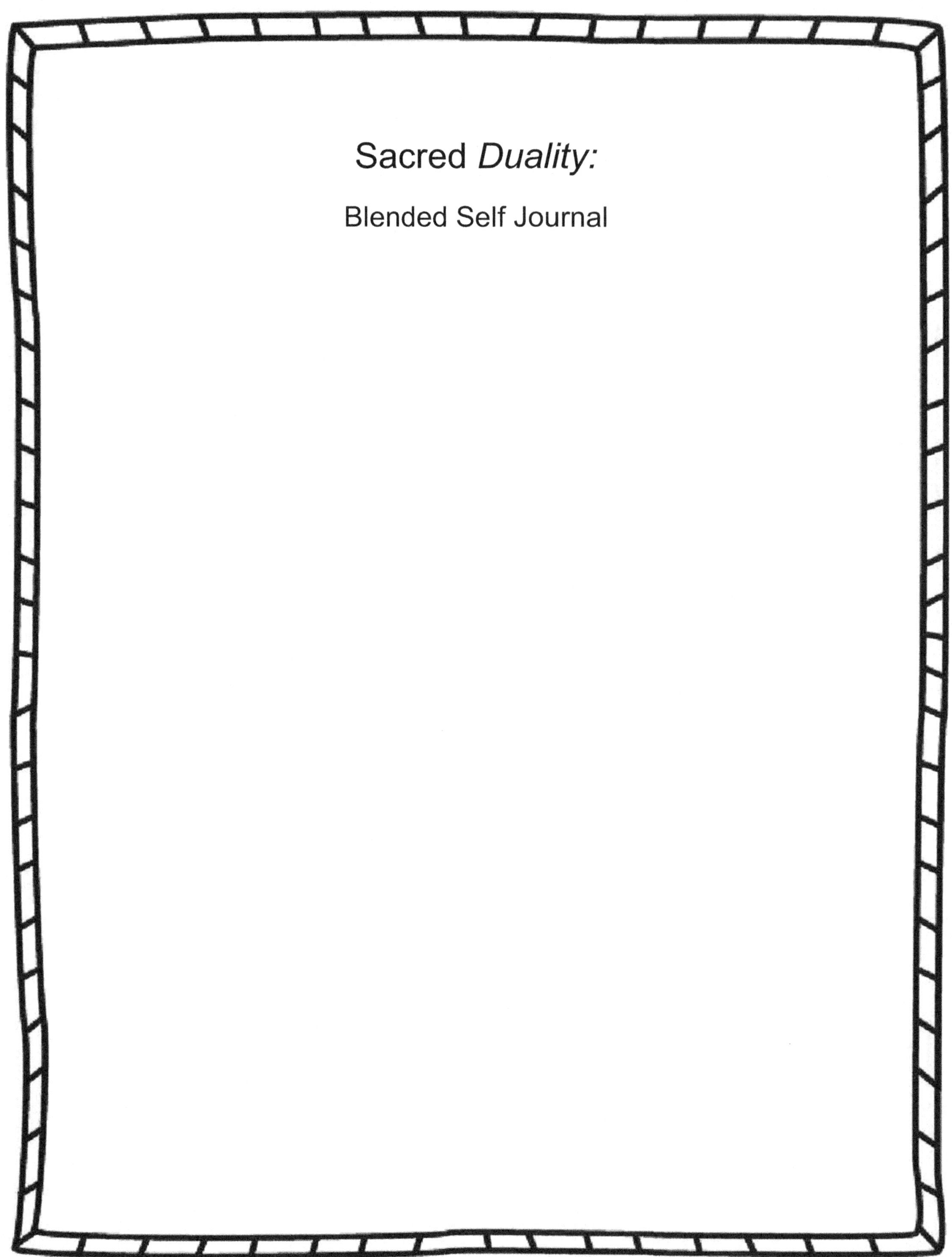
Sacred Duality:

Blended Self Journal

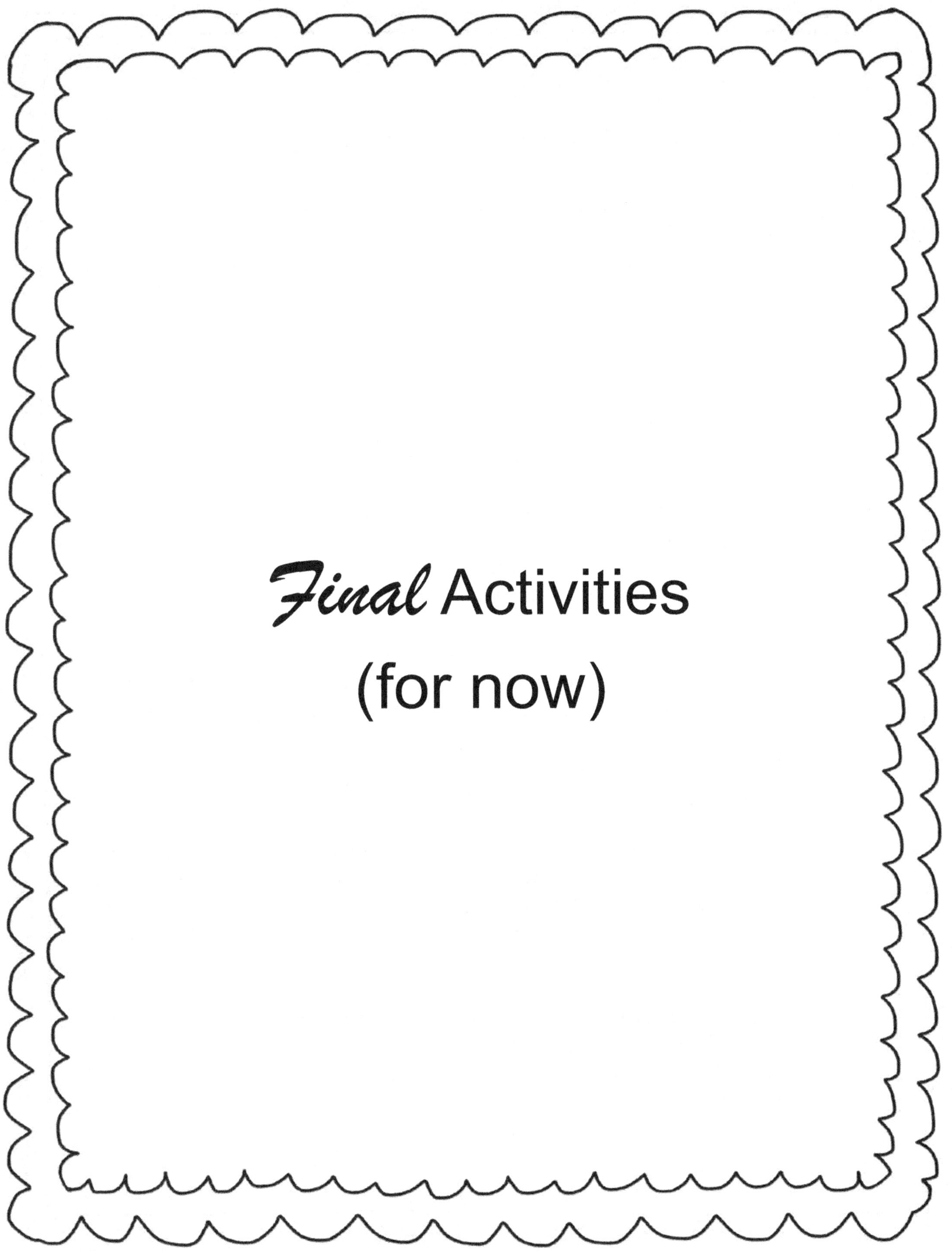

Final Activities
(for now)

A Month of *Affirmations!*

Affirmations are phrases that affirm our greatest needs and wishes. With so much negative talk and criticism within our minds, affirmations are a powerful balm that help us to feel more positive, secure, successful, and peaceful. Everything possesses magnetic energy—even our thoughts and words—and affirmations help attract goodness into our lives.

Write thirty positive affirmations that affirm the many wonderful discoveries you have made from using this workbook.

The best affirmations are written using the present tense so that we feel NOW as though the affirmation were already true. In this regard, "I am" is my favorite way to start nearly every affirmation, as in the following example: "I am free to be joyful and creative at all times." If I began the phrase with "I will be" instead of "I am," then my mind will think that there is more to pursue. And I'm tired of the pursuit! I'm ready to just BE! So, let our affirmations help with this.

Write your thirty affirmations on the next two pages. Take your time; there is no need to rush this exercise. Thirty may feel like a lot, but I believe that you have thirty loving and exciting things to say to yourself to counter the negative thoughts that you re-think so often. Your affirmations can feel a little silly, too! So I encourage you to push yourself. This exercise will actually help re-wire the old neurological pathways in your brain that have been made by your habitual negative self-talk.

When you're finished, you'll then do what you did with the thirty quotes. Cut each affirmation into a strip, fold it up, and put them all into a bowl. Place it in a special spot where you'll see it each morning, and intuitively choose one each day. Carry it with you throughout your day, and think of it often. You might wish to journal about it before you go to bed.

You are a beautiful being, inside and out. You are deserving NOW and always of abundant love, joy, success, and peace. You are a glowing creative spirit with so much to offer, and I wish you a blessed path on which your spirit will soar!

Thirty *Affirmations*...GO!

Write Your *Eulogy*

One day after we have lived life to the fullest our dear bodies will stop working. We will die, and then what happens next is the greatest mystery within our human awareness. I personally believe that my soul will leave my body and ascend to a higher place where it will prepare to reincarnate as another human being—all for the sake of my soul's ever-growing relationship to love.

I've heard it said that there is only one thing in life that we can be certain of, and that is death. If this is true, then how will you live your life today? How can your impending departure be a positive influence on what you do and who you are? How can death serve as your greatest source of inspiration?

For this exercise I invite you to write your own eulogy—the speech that a loved one delivers about your life at your funeral service. Your eulogy should honor and describe your accomplishments, personality, and values. It might also include anecdotal stories to illustrate an impression that you made on a friend or relative.

Writing your eulogy is a unique way of identifying your life's greatest goals. When all is said and done, for what do you wish to be remembered the most? What do you wish to leave behind? What truly matters to you?

This exercise may bring up uncomfortable feelings about death, such as fear or sadness. This is normal. So, take your time, and honor the feelings that emerge. I have provided journal prompts to help process your thoughts and feelings.

Here are some suggestions:

- Write with a sense of humor if that will help you to complete this exercise.

- Write your eulogy with a friend. Their presence and input may help you feel more supported as you do this exercise.

- Gather flowers, light a candle, and have a friend read your finished eulogy aloud to you. Honor your feelings as you listen to what is read.

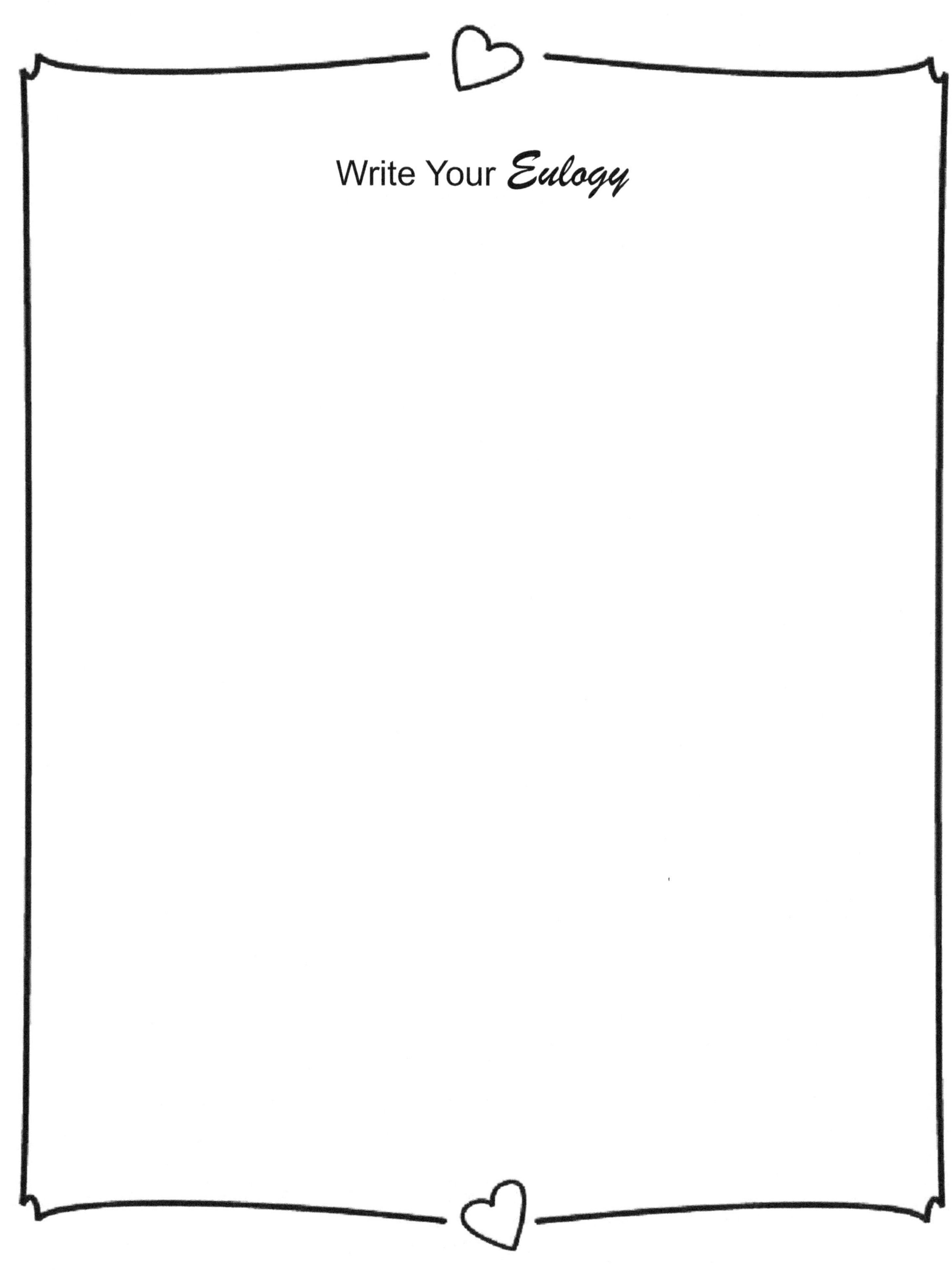

Write Your *Eulogy*

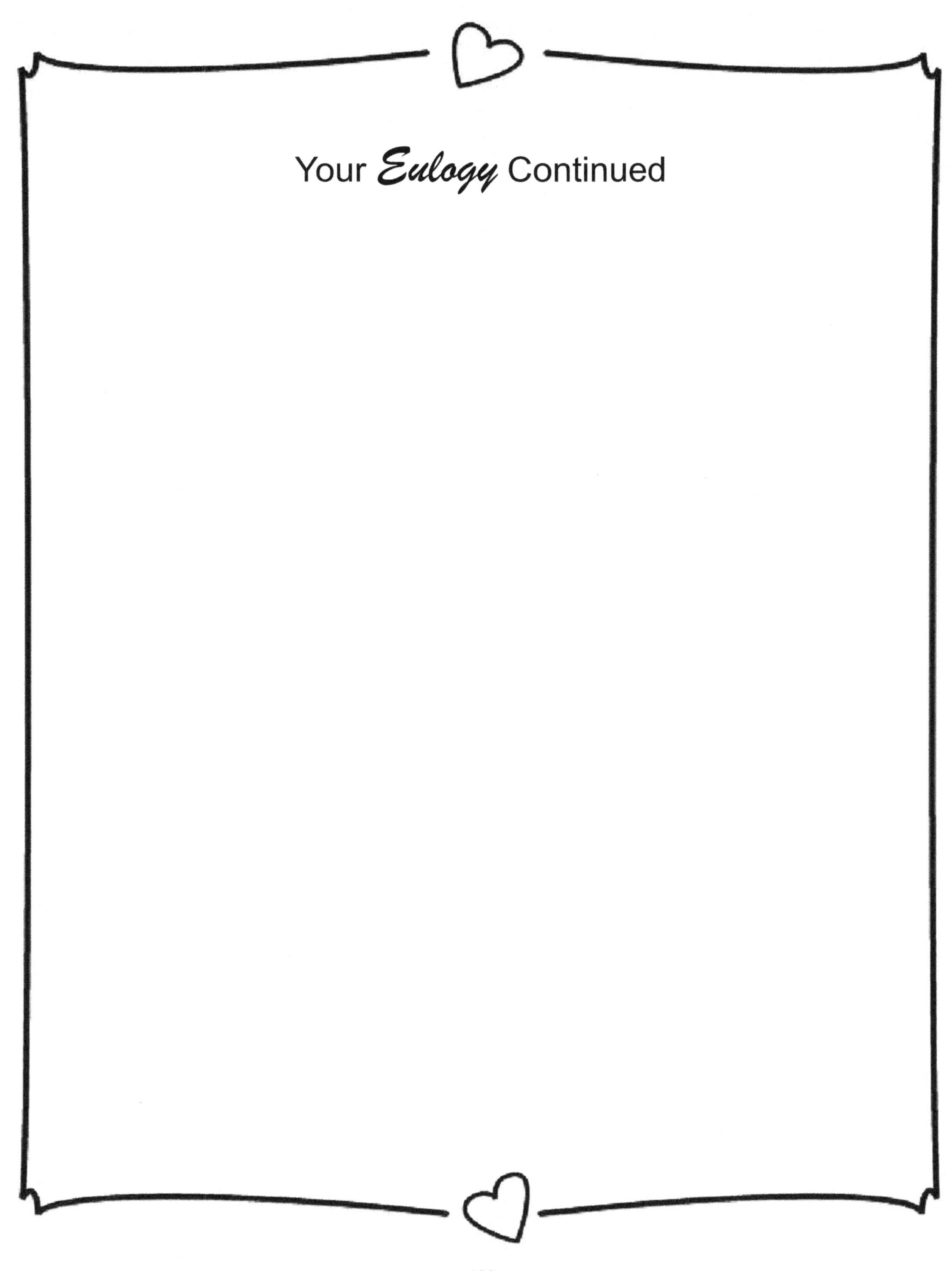

Your *Eulogy* Continued

Your *Eulogy* Journal

1. What are your thoughts and feelings about death?

2. Have you experienced the death of a loved one? How did their death affect how you live your own life?

3. How did their death affect your beliefs about death and dying?

4. How did it feel to write your eulogy?

5. Who would you like to have read your eulogy at your end of life ceremony? Why this person?

6. How does your eulogy inspire your life now?

7. If you were to die in one year/one week/one day, what would you create now?

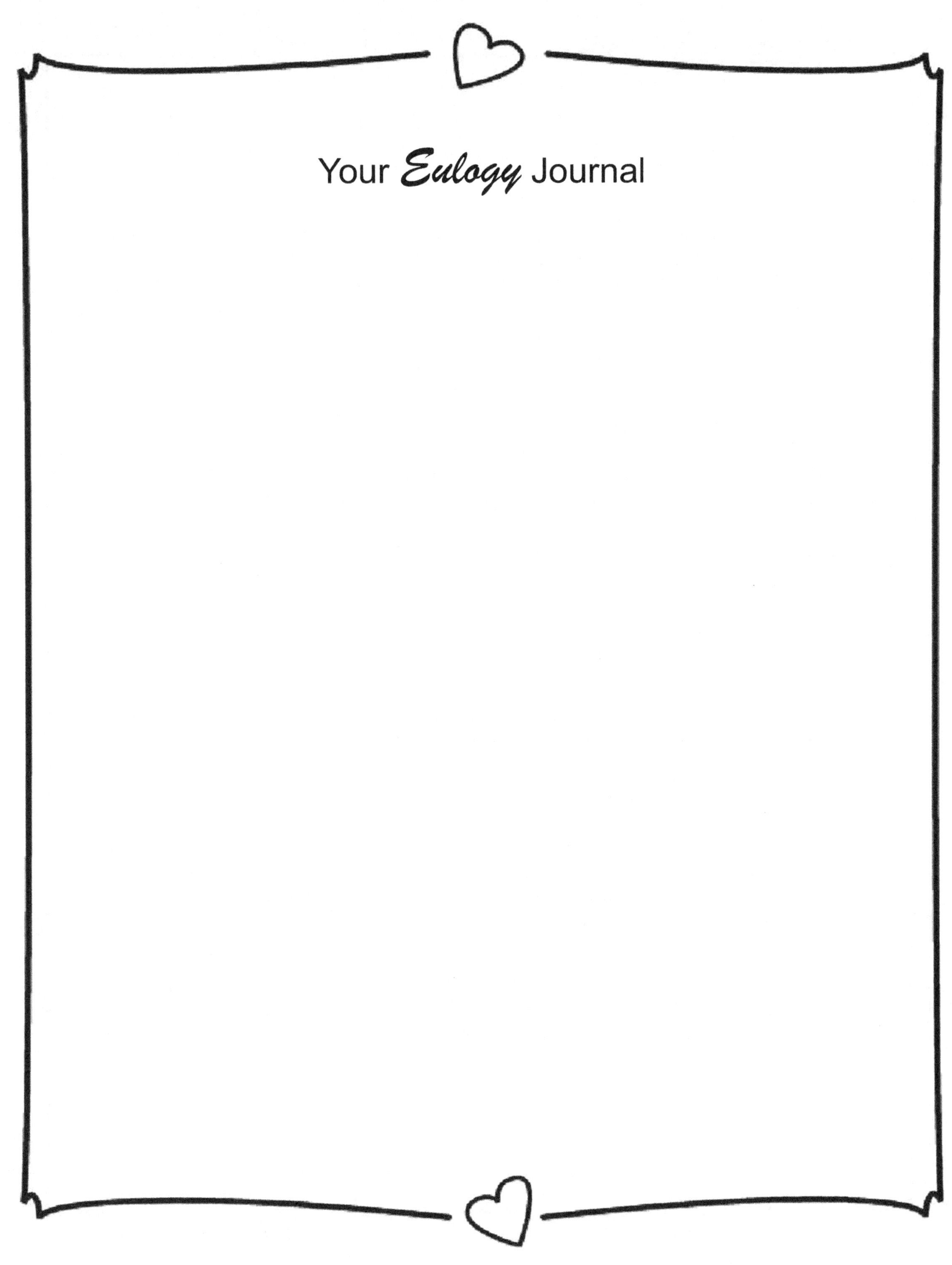

Your *Eulogy* Journal

Create Your Own *Ceremony!*

Ceremonies have been performed as long as humans have walked the earth. They are used to celebrate and honor special occasions and rites of passage, including births, deaths, and marriages. Weddings, funerals, and birthday parties are familiar examples of modern day ceremonies. The benefits of ceremony include growth and healing, building confidence, having fun or grieving, cultivating community, connecting with the invisible realms, and feeling empowered.

Ceremonies come in all shapes and sizes, and they are created for many purposes. Indigenous cultures perform healing ceremonies to create harmony and healing within the body. Native American youth go on a vision quest—a solo ceremony intended to help clarify one's life purpose. Vision quests also deal with the supernatural realm and help the child connect with their spirit guides. A Christian baptism inducts the person into the religion's faith, and followers of the Wiccan faith perform croning ceremonies for women and saging ceremonies for men. These are intended to initiate the woman or man into elderhood and their roles as wise leaders within their communities. And lastly, a coming out party celebrates the sexuality of a person within the LGBTQ+ community.

Ceremonies can be religious, spiritual or secular, big or small, extravagant or sparse, indoors or outdoors, long or short, and involve either hundreds of people or only one or two. The sky is the limit! They are incredible opportunities to get creative, get personal, and make occasions sacred and special.

My invitation to you: Plan and perform a ceremony for yourself that honors and celebrates the discoveries you have made by doing the exercises in this book. You have worked hard and explored deep within yourself! Now YOU are worth celebrating, either alone or with loved ones.

On the next page I share an outline created by my friend Michael Trotta of StoryMischief.com. His stages and my descriptions will provide you with a template for preparing a beautiful and meaningful ceremony. The outline is followed by some suggestions to help make your ceremony as fun and magical as possible!

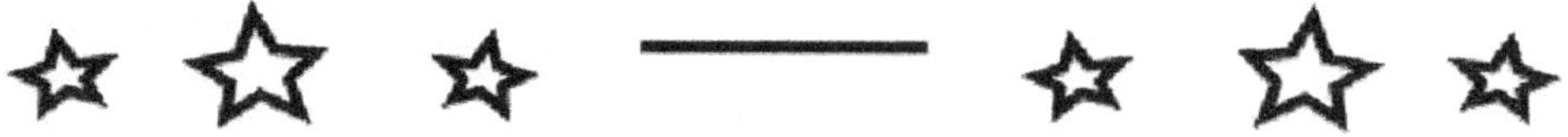

Ceremony Outline

Here is an outline of a ceremony's stages and sequence. Use this to plan what you'd like to do and say and what supplies you'd like to use in your ceremony.

INTENTION

- State out loud and share with others the intention (goal) of the ceremony. This stage can include prayers and invocations.

INSPIRATION

- an action to begin the ceremony, inspire participants, and set the mood (examples: lighting a candle, playing music, putting on a ceremonial costume, reading a poem)

PREPARATION

- preparing the space and participants for the ceremony's main activity (examples: short meditation, presenting supplies/sacred objects, sharing information and instructions)

PERSPIRATION

- the ceremony's main activity which embodies the intention (examples: delivering a speech, performing a dance or dramatic scene, writing something meaningful and safely burning it)

RELAXATION

- a short moment of rest after the main activity (examples: group breath, a moment of silence, bathroom break, musical interlude)

CELEBRATION

- praising the experience, each other, and the effort (examples: enjoying food and drink, dancing, hugs and conversation)

REFLECTION

- processing what happened and what emerged during the ceremony (examples: talking circle, journaling)

INTEGRATION

- incorporating the ceremony's effects and learnings into your daily life and thereby remaining conscious of the ceremony's magic.

Ceremony Suggestions

An Exciting Purpose: Your ceremony's purpose should honor something about yourself that really excites you. Inspired by the exercises in the workbook, you could create a ceremony that honors your Soul Powers, sacred duality, creative spirit, coming out, merging of your inner child and older self, new ways of self care, and your inner mythic hero.

Gather Your Loved Ones: If you wish to include friends and relatives in your ceremony, their presence can be very powerful. They will serve as loving witnesses to the emergence of your new self. Create invitations and notify your guests in advance. And be sure to include them in the ceremony's activities! Your musician friend should bring his guitar, and your writer friend should definitely read their poetry!

Mix and Match: The ceremony stages can be re-arranged and blended together in ways that only you can imagine! There is no right or wrong way to plan. You are the master of your ceremony so be as creative as you'd like!

Sacred Objects and Decor: I LOVE creating mood and atmosphere. If you desire, decorate your space with special items that help create an air of magic. Manipulate the lighting, and gather beautiful objects that support your ceremony's intention. You can be as lavish or as simple as you wish.

Dress Up: Costumes are a traditional element in most ceremonies. Think about the minister who wears his robe or the bride who wears her gown. What you wear has meaning and supports the ceremony's intention. So, dress up! Celebrating your creative spirit or sacred duality? Have fun planning those costumes. And invite your guests to dress up, as well!

Reflection and Integration: The Come Out journal in this workbook includes excellent questions that you can use to process your ceremony.

And Have Fun! Need I say more? Even a grief ceremony can have moments of lightness and levity.

Blessings on your beautiful and transformational ceremony!

Start a *Soaring Spirits Circle!*

Using this workbook privately will reap many personal benefits, as will doing the exercises with a group of like-hearted seekers. Consider forming a Soaring Spirits Circle! Group members can provide support and encouragement for one another as you engage with the work together. Here are some suggestions on how to structure a welcoming, productive, and magical Soaring Spirits Circle:

1. Devote your first meeting to making group-based decisions about your circle's structure, schedule, and goals.

2. Decide when you will use the workbook: during meetings or between meetings, or both?

3. Shared facilitation of meetings is a nice way to structure leadership. This way, the responsibility does not fall on one member's shoulders. Members can take turns opening and closing meetings.

4. Create a welcoming and safe environment by establishing basic rules. Confidentiality is a good one to maintain. I also like to implement a 'no cross talk' rule. This means that there are to be no interruptions with questions or comments while someone is sharing. Reserve responses and feedback (if requested) for later.

5. Make your meetings sacred. Begin meetings with a short meditation or by stating an intention. Similarly, close the meeting in a special way that honors what has emerged during the session.

6. Have fun and enjoy the rewarding experience of connecting with fellow creative spirits!

I wish your circle much success! Feel free to contact me, Peyton, for more ideas and support for starting your own Soaring Spirits Circle. You may contact me through my website: www.creativespiritma.com.

Made in the USA
Middletown, DE
09 April 2022

63937861R00077